Adrienne Auslander Munich

Andromeda's Chains

GENDER AND INTERPRETATION IN VICTORIAN LITERATURE AND ART

Columbia University Press
NEW YORK

COLUMBIA UNIVERSITY PRESS
NEW YORK CHICHESTER, WEST SUSSEX

LIBRARY OF CONGRESS CATALOGING IN-PUBLICATION DATA

Munich, Adrienne.
Andromeda's chains : gender and interpretation in Victorian literature and art / Adrienne Auslander Munich.
p. cm.
Bibliography : p.
Includes index.
ISBN *0-231-06872-7*
ISBN *0-231-06873-5 (pbk.)*
1. Arts, Victorian—Great Britain.
2. Arts, British.
3. Allegories.
4. Women in art.
5. Andromeda (Greek mythology)—Art.
6. Perseus (Greek mythology)—Art.
7. Feminism and literature—Great Britian.
I. Title.
NX543.M86 1989
700'.941—dc19
88-34077
CIP
∞

Printed in the United States of America

Casebound editions of Columbia University Press books are printed on permanent and durable acid-free paper.

For Myra

Contents

Illustrations

Acknowledgments

N MY use of feminist discourse developed over the last fifteen years I am gratefully dependent upon those critics who have charted the territory, articulating what previously was unprintable and empowering many others. More directly I thank the Women's Studies Faculty Development Seminar at Yale University, particularly Nancy Cott, who bridged institutional boundaries to welcome me. After those sessions, Christine Froula and I debated theoretical positions for hours until, together, we knew what we thought. The Yale Center for British Art provided a fellowship and continuing resources, the Stony Brook English Department relieved me of teaching responsibilities, and the State University of New York awarded me two summer research grants. The Beinecke Library,

Sterling Memorial Library at Yale University, and the Warburg Institute Library at the University of London made available their resources and their able staffs to me. Particular thanks to Betty Muirden, librarian at the Yale Center for British Art.

The audiences for talks at the Center for Independent Study, the Yale Center for British Art, the MLA Convention, the Victorian Committee Seminar at the CUNY Graduate Center, and the Stony Brook English Department responded with stimulating and appropriate questions. I thank those who read and commented on parts of the manuscript: Susan Casteras, Margaret Ferguson, Christine Froula, Rachel Jacoff, Coppélia Kahn, George Landow, David Laurence, Marlon Ross, Sallie Sears, Carole Silver, Patricia Spacks, and Susan Squier. Patricia Spacks made writing possible by giving me rare, generous intellectual hospitality and by escaping from work with me at opportune moments. John Hollander steadfastly believed in the value of my work. Two readers for the Columbia University Press provided an astute and generative audience at a point where I believed I could have no more ideas on the subject; Jennifer Crewe receives my warm praise for selecting them and for her confidence in the manuscript. She and other editors at Columbia, such as Joan McQuary, made me happily aware of our collaborative venture.

In addition to reading most drafts, Richard Munich provided solace and encouragement while my writing changed our lives. I could not have written this book without the men in my family, Richard, Edwin, and Matthew, who allowed me to participate in their continuing struggles for and against the gender economy. As I wrote I dreamed of my sister Myra, who died sweetly and quietly, wearing her chains, to whom this book is dedicated.

ANDROMEDA'S CHAINS

Are there objects which are *inevitably* a source of suggestiveness, as Baudelaire suggested about Woman? Certainly not: one can conceive of very ancient myths, but there are not eternal ones; for it is human history which converts reality to speech, and it alone rules the life and the death of mythical language. Ancient or not, mythology can only have an historical foundation, for myth is a type of speech chosen by history; it cannot possibly evolve from the 'nature' of things.

ROLAND BARTHES, *Mythologies*

So long as an opinion is strongly rooted in the feelings, it gains rather than loses in stability by having a preponderating weight of argument against it . . . And there are so many causes tending to make the feeling connected with this subject the most intense and most deeply-rooted of all those which gather round and protect old institutions and customs, that we need not wonder to find them as yet less undermined and loosened than any of the rest by the progress of the great modern spiritual and social transition nor suppose that the barbarisms to which men cling longest must be less barbarisms than those which they earlier shake off.

J. S. MILL, "On the Subjection of Women"

INTRODUCTION

Interpretation and Gender

THIS BOOK explores the power and the passion with which male writers and artists from the 1830s to the 1890s gave meaning to the Perseus and Andromeda myth and its cognate, St. George and the dragon. I am interested in the reasons for the Victorian fascination with the myth, the interpretative methods used to produce divergent meanings, and the cultural implications of Victorian interpretations from the vantage of twentieth-century criticism. Each Victorian representation transforms the myth so that the composite picture over the sixty-year period, like theme and variations, yields apparently irreconcilable meanings. It is precisely this multiplicity that makes the study of Victorian Andromedas revealing—of cultural complexity and of a culture's ways of incorporating what it cannot confront directly.

While I did not initially think of Andromeda myth as gender-specific in its attractions, I discovered that men rather than women employed the Perseus and Andromeda myth for their creative uses and that considerations of gender played a major role in their interpretations of it. For that reason an analysis of Victorian Andromedas illuminates a gendered aspect of Victorian culture. Subsequent chapters will demonstrate ways that the Perseus and Andromeda myth became a coded account of male conflicts about the sex/gender system of their times. When considered as a paradigm more hospitable to male than to female interpretation, Victorian versions of the Perseus and Andromeda myth expose the politics of cultural reconstruction of gender within the process of its representation. But individual interpretations at once reinscribe conventional gender categories and subvert them, expressing personal fears and desires. Men used the Andromeda myth not only to celebrate the rewards of a patriarchal system but also to record their discomforts with it.

Feminist criticism of the Victorian era has revised our view of the age by reexamining women's writing, by paying serious attention to heretofore discounted women writers, and by opening new directions of critical inquiry. But, by focusing attention on women's cultural productions, much of this criticism has conveyed a mistaken impression that gender issues concerned women more than men. On the contrary, men as much as women express concerns about fundamental changes in social organization in relation to gender. Tracts by men about femininity, such as the politically divergent responses by Ruskin and Mill, could be considered as a convert acknowledgment of new kinds of disturbances in the gender system. One way men avoided a possibly threatening autobiographical response to social change was by focusing on femininity and on explorations of women's capacities and proper social role. Charles Kingsley, a telling example, delivers a little-known feminine treatise, "Triumph of Woman," in his novel *Yeast,* discussed in chapter 2. Because Kingsley's portrayal of womanly essence is embedded in a loosely constructed novel addressing the contemporary scene, the fantasy behind it and the disquiet that fantasy attempts to control is made detectable, suggesting the possibility that similar disturbances are masked by other male writing about women, such as Ruskin's mythopoesis in "Of Queen's Gardens" and the prescriptive sentiments of Patmore's *The Angel in the House*.

The sacred precincts of Victorian classical learning, off-limits to most Victorian women because of exclusionary educational policies, has not benefited from contemporary feminist cultural critique. My method in this study applies feminist analysis to one aspect of the Victorian classical revival—male writers and artists who treated the Perseus and Andromeda legend. Early feminist writing which examined male authored texts from the perspective of gender discovered misogyny and its polemics of representation, but gender tensions revealed in Victorian representations of this myth cannot be so simply, or so negatively, categorized. One discovers envy, fear, curiosity, unease, as well as a conservative effort to classify women as docile Andromedas and men as stalwart Perseuses. One cannot assume that men always identify themselves in male roles; some men, either overtly or symbolically, imagine themselves as Andromeda. My method has been to balance a consideration of psychological and cultural aspects in various representations of a single myth. Most of the works I discuss have received little critical attention, although most of the authors and painters are well known. To turn feminist inquiry to Victorian male authors and painters as they reimagine a classical story alters our view of their more familiar work. To make available what is generally disregarded casts a different light on what is taken as tradition, sometimes with discomfitting results. My effort will, I hope, suggest similar investigations in other areas. Not only by adding more women to the canon but also by illuminating its dark corners do we change cultural history.

As in all critical inquiry, I am interested in interpretation, but my perspective interrogates the processes of interpretation as well as the meanings derived from them. Feminist inquiry, reflecting on the ideologies which are integral to established interpretative methods, allows us to question hermeneutic methods and to discern the politics of their authority.[1] The myth not only speaks to and for the age, but it also speaks in different voices. Those voices and the hermeneutic traditions which allow them to be heard are as implicated in the gender economy as are the meanings derived from them. The metaphors that produce meaning reveal gender-marked assumptions which close off possible meanings as they disclose others.

Although discourse about the ancients evokes a world of ostensibly universal, gender-neutral values, metaphors and locutions about classical studies address a male audience, often with specifically male concerns. Victorians were aware that classical revivals, particularly in the arts, reflected the contemporary concerns of the age, not necessarily those of the antique past. With the interpretative process closed to women, articles in Victorian periodicals discuss the age's reinvention of classicism as an opening of old myths to new meanings but nonetheless reinscribe male privilege in their mythology.[2] A. H. Sayce, professor of Assyriology and colleague of the linguist Max Müller at Oxford, unconsciously evoked a male world of classical studies when he observed that an age has vested interests in its revivals: "The myth takes its coloring from each generation that repeats it, and clothes it with the passions and the interests and the knowledge of the men in whose mouths it lives and grows."[3] Sayce addresses a community of men for whom these myths have particular meaning; his locution includes gender in its consideration. What were those male passions, interests, and knowledge which inspired the classical revival? Sayce does not mention them.

Describing the motive for retelling classical myths as an "inversion of homesickness,"[4] Walter Pater, like Sayce, assumed a learned milieu in which men reconsider the classics according to their own particular, historically determined biases, but he also suggests a gendered arena of male desire fueling the interest in the antique world. Reviewing William Morris' use of Greek material, including the entire Perseus story in *The Earthly Paradise,* the critic confronted the cultural meaning of revivals in a passage worth quoting in its entirety:

> In handling a subject of Greek legend, anything in the way of an actual revival must always be impossible. Such vain antiquarianism is a waste of the poet's power. The composite experience of all the ages is part of each one of us: to deduct from that experience to obliterate any part of it, to come face to face

> with the people of a past age, as if the middle age, the Renaissance, the eighteenth century had not been, is as impossible as to become a little child, or enter again into the womb and be born. But though it is not possible to repress a single phase of that humanity, which, because we live and move and have our being in the life of humanity, makes us what we are; it is possible to isolate such a phase, to throw it into relief, to be divided against ourselves in zeal for it, as we may hark back to some choice space of our own individual life. We cannot truly conceive the age: we can conceive the element it has contributed to our culture; we can treat the subjects of the age bringing that into relief. Such an attitude towards Greece, aspiring to but never actually reaching its way of conceiving life, is what is possible for art.[5]

Pater's maternal metaphor animates the dynamic between a traditionally male subject and the unrecoverable maternal object of desire, a desire mediated by years of fantasy and inevitable disappointment. He suggests that the male yearning for the past, expressed by retelling a Greek story, is like the yearning to return to the womb. Both are desires by their nature unappeasable and creative. Echoing yet paganizing Christ's metaphor of conversion as regression to childhood, Pater makes the return more concrete, more specifically linked to the mother. Like the vexed desire for maternal union, the appeal of the ancient story confirms an alienation from it. Individual life and classical revival have a common ground, a mutual desire. With the double meaning of "conceive" echoing through the passage like an insistent refrain, Pater suggests the conflict which fueled Victorian males to create their own Andromeda myths, divided from yet inextricably connected to the past by the cord we identify as Western tradition. He suggests not so much an inverted as a primal version of homesickness—desire for the womb.

Pater not only connects the desire to retell a classical story with the desire to return to a maternal origin, he also indicates a way of speculating about the motivating passion for such a desire. Linking the matrix of thought to the womb, Pater's figurative language suggests that curiosity about gender formation is one major interest in classical revivals.[6] By identifying momentarily with a classical myth, an artist leaps backward into the womb of civilization when the origins of the gender arrangements in the Western world were being mythologized, reconceiving the importance of that binary arrangement of the sexes for his own times. The Victorian might wish to erase the intervening centuries separating his own age from the ancients in order to obliterate the changes in gender relations, returning to the way he imagined gender relations in the ancient world. He might imagine this past as more or less tolerant of a variety of sexual behavior. As Pater explains it, no matter what the form of a Victorian revivalists's fantasy about life in the golden age of Greece, the effort to imagine the distant past as if the more proximate past, or, indeed, the present, had not occurred requires an inner split, revealing an imaginative fault-line. From the perspective of a later age and with an interest in exploring rather than confirming Victorian ideas, a twentieth-century critic can point out those splits in representation, revealing the Victorian gender conflicts that male desire for maternal origins implies.[7] Victorian interpretative traditions themselves disclose the interpreters' desires.

Why this particular myth at that particular time? Chapter 1 begins with some Romantic antecedents and then surveys a series of Victorian examples to suggest the limits of a possible answer. The examples chart a poetics tied to the theme of rescue and to characters who assume polarized gender roles. To compare a Romantic myth of bondage and rescue with a Victorian one makes concrete a historical change in sensibility and concerns, suggesting the social context producing the quickened interest in the Andromeda myth and the diversity of its interpretations.

Hermeneutic methods, themselves gender-marked, provide the tools by which individuals derive and validate their meanings. Chapters 2, 3, and 4 examine three hermeneutic methods—allegorical, typological, and emblematic—and the artists and writers who employed them. Devoted to close exegesis, each of these chapters starts roughly at the beginning of the sixty years—in the 30s or 40s—and finishes toward the end, with chapter 2 ending in 1869 and chapter 4 covering the widest span: from 1833 to 1895. Rather than charting a chronological development (I do not find any progressive change during the sixty years), each chapter focuses on different methods of interpretation and thus juxtaposes figures one might not otherwise consider together. In discussing interpretative methods, I recognize that, much like tropes, they tend to overlap and blend. They are useful heuristically to map general territories, but even the most simple Victorian interpretation overflows the categories of my critical inquiry. I have chosen to allow my inquiry to chart these blendings and weavings, sacrificing classical balance to Victorian electicism. The result, I hope, is a more accurate picture of the Victorian processes of making meaning.

It is possible, however, to define general limits of interpretative methods and to describe what sorts of interpretations they tend to encourage, all with implications for gender construction. Allegories create a rational distance between interpretation and representation, separating abstract meaning from concrete representation. Victorians use allegorical interpretation to moralize the myth, making its meaning abstract while at the same time dwelling on the representation of physical pain. Typological interpretation makes parallel narratives from biblical and classical sources. This interpretative method promotes a merging of difference, transgressing boundaries between different kinds of stories, but also, as I argue in chapter 3, encouraging the blurring of other conventionally firm boundaries, such as those separating the genders. Emblems, coded pictures whose meanings are available only to those initiated into the mystery of a specific pictographic system, claim a powerful territory outside the boundary of language. That territory has been culturally marked as the realm of the female. While methods of interpretation limit the meanings one can derive, their very conventionality enabled some Victorian men to explore and question fixed genders and established power hierarchies without seeming particularly revolutionary. Traditional strategies of interpretation, used to tell a familiar myth, provide a cover for more subversive stories, counter-tales encoded in transformations of an ancient myth. In making many different meanings from a myth with a particular attraction during a sixty-year period, Victorian Andromedas, all of them bound and many of them rescued, create a richly diverse sign of the times.

CHAPTER ONE

The Poetics of Rescue, The Politics of Bondage

WHEN WILLIAM Etty (1787–1845), whose career stands at a transition in English cultural history, painted a Prometheus (1825–30?, figure 1.1), he was interpreting the myth that the second generation Romantics embraced as a heroic sign.[1] Although the painting takes its theme from the Titan as interpreted by Lord Byron, Mary Shelley, and Percy Shelley, Etty's Prometheus presents a different vision, one emphasizing punishment and pain rather than defiance. Byron's 1816 Prometheus may be closest to Etty's, but, unlike the painter, the poet celebrates the Titan's triumph, not his downfall:

> Thou art a symbol and a sign
> To Mortals of their fate and force . . .

To which his Spirit may oppose
Itself—an equal to all woes,
And a firm will, and a deep sense,
Which even in torture can descry
Its own concentered recompense,
Triumphant where it dares defy,
And making Death a Victory.[2]

Percy Shelley's Prometheus challenged Jupiter; incorruptible despite his tortures, he championed mankind, resisting injustice without compromise. Shelley drew parallels between Christ and Prometheus, finding in his hero "the type of the highest perfection of moral and intellectual nature, impelled by the purest and the truest motives to the best and noblest ends."[3] Even Mary

1.1. William Etty, *Prometheus*
Reproduced by permission of National Museums and Galleries on Merseyside.

Shelley's more subversive view, critical of the narcissistic male ambition fueling male overachievement, portrays a "Modern Prometheus," Dr. Frankenstein, as failing due to grand audacity in attempting to imitate creation, whether woman's ability to give birth or divine power to create life from clay.

In contrast, Etty's Prometheus, a muscular titan of a man, has been felled by an arrow. One leg, still manacled, remains chained to a rock; his outstretched arms resemble the pose of a crucified Christ or, with the arrow piercing his ribs, a Christian martyr such as St. Sebastian. Etty's foreshorted figure, head downward, assumes the pose not of Christ but of St. Peter, who wished to be crucified upside down as a sign of his inferiority to Christ. Unlike Shelley's unbound Prometheus, whose sufferings attain cosmic reconciliation rather than unredeemed agony, Etty's partially bound Titan appears defeated. Etty has altered the myth, making Prometheus look as if the wound to his side were fatal, or, as the catalogue entry suggests, as if he were "transfixed." Hercules, his liberator, shot with an arrow the griffin-vulture who gnawed at the Titan's liver. The arrow may be symbolic both of Promethean torment and sacrifices for humanity, but Etty's martyred Prometheus conveys in his pose a suggestion of bondage rather than martyrdom. His arms and the one unbound leg seem almost languid, lending a luxuriousness to his supine body, extending to his one manacled muscular limb. Etty's Prometheus yields to voluptuous coma in his questionable triumph.

As St. Peter to Christ, so Etty's Prometheus to the figure imagined by Byron and the Shelleys. A change in sensibility lies in the ratio. Whereas the Prometheus myth seemed an apt way to figure the late Romantic poets' challenge to human oppression, it failed to offer Victorian poets and painters a similarly inspiring plot, passing instead to Karl Marx as a fit emblem for workers against powerful oppressors.[4]

More telling in Victorian representation than the change from a Christlike Prometheus to a Peter-like one is the change from worship of Prometheus to elevation of Andromeda as a device for the times. In a wide range of Victorian representations Andromeda, another figure from Greek mythology chained to a rock and threatened by divinely mandated creatures, replaces the chained

Titan. Again, the difference between Andromeda and Prometheus denotes a cultural shift, a transformation of a Romantic theme. In 1819, the same year that Shelley published *Prometheus Unbound,* Keats wrote "On the Sonnet," a poem using Andromeda as a personification of poetic form:

> If by dull rhymes our English must be chain'd,
> And, like Andromeda, the Sonnet sweet
> Fetter'd, in spite of pained loveliness;
> Let us find out, if we must be constrain'd,
> Sandals more interwoven and complete
> To fit the naked foot of Poesy;
> Let us inspect the lyre, and weigh the stress
> Of every chord, and see what may be gain'd
> By ear industrious, and attention meet;
> Misers of sound and syllable, no less
> Than Midas of his coinage, let us be
> Jealous of dead leaves in the bay-wreath crown;
> So, if we may not let the Muse be free,
> She will be bound with garlands of her own.[5]

Dissatisfied with a form imported from the continent and unsuited to the English language, Keats sought not to emancipate the form into free verse but to find more native limits. Although Keats writes of the English sonnet, he also implies that the Andromeda myth does not free the maiden but licenses her more meetly. Rather than liberating Andromeda into her own freely chosen life, she is given more accommodating bonds in union with her own kind.

Keats' sonnet was published in 1848, the year Dante Gabriel Rossetti wrote his sonnets on the romance adaptation of the Andromeda myth by Ariosto—Ruggiero freeing Angelica—and fifteen years after Robert Browning in *Pauline* described Andromeda as his Muse. By that time Etty left at least four canvases depicting the myth. The bound Titan becomes a bound mortal Princess, an indication of a new kind of attention to women and, more profoundly, a recognition of revolutionary movement in the social sphere alloted to them. Furthermore, it was not women but men artists and writers who imagined and represented the fettered woman. As the ensuing discussion will argue, Victorian representations of Andromeda imply a politics of interpretation, a politics affecting gender arrangements of a society undergoing vast social changes, not the least of which was the solidification of separate gendered spheres and challenges to that separation.

Many Victorians represent Andromeda's rescue in the context of other rescue plots, but unlike William Ewart Gladstone, who attempted to save fallen women from the actual streets of sin, or Aurora Leigh and Romola who rescue abused outcast women into the haven of women's communities, Andromeda is virginal, with neither sin nor volition. Not a victim of the economic system but possibly a captive of racist and colonial fantasies, she is an Ethiopian or Arabian princess who became exceptionally interesting as a subject for male middle-class writers and artists who represented Andromeda—along with Perseus and the monster—with the passion their antecedents devoted to Prometheus. To wonder why they did so requires an examination of what meanings they found in the story they received—primarily from Ovid or from romance versions of the St. George legend—and how they arrived at those meanings.

The myth's melodramatic plot ranges the three main characters on an absolute moral scale. A vulnerable, naked, and blameless maiden, chained to a rock by her parents, is about to be eaten by a monster. The crusading hero has just killed the Medusa with divine aid when he chances upon the maiden, saves her by vanquishing the monster, and marries her. The myth ends with Perseus ceding his throne to his oldest son, who establishes either the Persian or the Mycenaean nation. As a permanent memorial to the significance of their story, the main characters are translated into the firmament as constellations.

The hero's story begins with his supernatural engendering by Zeus, disguised as a shower of gold, continues through his subsequent difficulties with his mother's suitor, and ends with the characters' apotheosis. Before Perseus can marry and reproduce, he must sever the Medusa's head. Most of the Victorians represent the adventure after the hero has killed Medusa, when he readies himself to slay the dragon and unbind the maiden. From the point of view of his development, that powerful moment depicts a transitional period, experienced as greatly threatening and momentous. Slaying the monster is the hero's final test of manhood before entering adult sexuality and joining the patriarchal hierarchy as founder of a dynasty, given greater historical status because he is also founding a nation.

In Victorian England the legend of St. George and the dragon is an analogue to the mythological rescue scene, the hero transformed to a knight of chivalric romance, with the additional attraction that St. George is the patron saint of England. Although the most familiar image is of two rather than three figures—St. George slaying a dragon—many English Victorian representations favor the version of the myth where the Saint kills the dragon then marries Princess Sabra. The Princess has unaccountably dressed as a bride when she goes to be eaten by the dragon, her wedding gown suggesting a rivalry between the monster and the saint.[6] Arrayed for her bridal, the Princess also dresses for a sacrifice analogous to or symbolic of marriage.

Andromeda, daughter of King Cepheus and Queen Casseopeia of Joppa, has no story, but she has a role and a lineage. Not exhibiting any personal pride in her extraordinary loveliness, she suffers because her mother boasted that her daughter's beauty surpassed that of the immortals. Her tears, like those of Penelope, Niobe, and countless women mourners, inspire pity and heroic deeds in men while expressing female helplessness and loss. Like a personification, she also possesses attributes: chains, nakedness, flowing hair, beauty, virginity. Without a voice in her fate, she neither defies the gods nor chooses her mate.

In the sense that the Andromeda myth took the fancy not of women but of men artists during the years between 1830 and 1895, it can be thought of as a male myth. Its polarized gender roles present a structural paradigm for an unequal distribution of power ostensibly favoring men. Interpreting the structure, the Victorian men examined here not only represent but also ratify traditional allocation of power according to gender. The creation of gender itself implies not only differences but also—to use Catharine MacKinnon's formulation—"the erotization of dominance and submission."[7] MacKinnon's summary of gender creation applies to the Andromeda myth, which both represents and constructs its plot according to the gendered erotics of power. It terms position a female with no power, seemingly with no volition, opposite a male with supernatural powers. In addition, the story serves heroic ambition. Perseus saves Andromeda, then keeps her for sexual and dynastic purposes; obligated to her rescuer, she can neither rescue herself nor refuse his offer of marriage.

Before giving close attention in subsequent chapters to three specific hermeneutic methods by which writers and artists constructed personal meanings from the Andromeda myth, I wish here to examine some Victorian examples of the creation of gender according to erotic dominance and submission, focusing on the three main figures: Perseus, Andromeda, and the monster.

The Poetics of Rescue: Perseus

RESCUE FANTASIES, a staple of everyday dream life, frequently follow simple narrative lines that hide the complexity of individual motives. Labeling the rescue fantasy universal and oedipal, Bruno Bettelheim asserts, "no little boy has ever failed to see himself in this starring role."[8] Although for grown men of the Victorian period, even men of reason and probity, rescue fantasies assume the dual aspect of private fantasy and national (even nationalistic) obsession, an examination of different Victorian representations of Perseus in the context of other Victorian rescue fantasies makes a problem rather than a blessing of that starring male role. In the sense in which one can consider the Andromeda myth as a male rescue fantasy, a personal plot, its rescue theme lends itself to psychological analysis. But the reiteration of what might seem a private fantasy also requires cultural analysis when it is shared, passed around as an agreed-upon tale, transmitted from one man to another, painted and written and confessed to. Thus, the Andromeda myth becomes a Victorian tradition.

"I wish I had been born in the days of Ogres and Dragon-guarded Castles," Charles Dickens confessed at age forty-five, constructing a rescue plot in a letter to his friend Lavinia Watson. She was the Lady of Rockingham Castle, the original of Chesney Wold in *Bleak House,* a place which might have been designed to foster such fantasies:[9]

> I wish an Ogre with seven heads . . . had taken the Princess whom I adore—you have no idea how intensely I love her!—to his stronghold on top of a high series of mountains, and there tied her up by the hair. Nothing would suit me half so well this day, as climbing after her, sword in hand, and either winning her or being killed.—*There's* a frame of mind for you, in 1857.[10]

Dickens' hyperbole expresses the extreme of his own condition: the ogre has seven heads; his love is beyond adoration; the hero must scale not one but a series of mountains. Such multiple barriers to winning the maiden or to the ultimate release from all heroics in death suggests a multiplicity of interpretations, moral and psychological. In addition to exaggerating the creature's oral aggressiveness, the ogre's seven heads suggest a biblical number. Like deadly sins, the heads might represent the traditional moral prohibitions preventing consummation of forbidden desire. Dickens imagined his rescue plot at a time in his life when he was particularly defenseless. He had just met Ellen Ternan, the young woman who was the catalyst for his separation from his wife. Written the year before his separation and emotional breakdown,[11] Dickens' rescue fantasy may express his own need of rescue, projecting his feelings of peril onto the maiden, at once object of his adoration and victim needing release.[12] His desire to escape domestic unhappiness becomes transformed into the conventional rescue scene, distanced in time from the harsh industrial realities of 1857 and also significantly distanced by the difference in gender. By making the imagined victim female rather than male and insisting on his own heroic role, Dickens disguises personal needs. Like Sherlock Holmes' Dr. Watson, the sympathetic Mrs. Watson provides a credulous and nurturant audience for the constructor of nefarious plots.

Dickens' fantasy barely masks its sadism; in spite of his protestations of self-transcendent love, he imagines the maiden as shackled by her own hair. The author punishes the lady in peril while casting himself both as knight and as victim: "I am the modern embodiment of the old Enchanters, whose Familiars tore them to pieces," the passage begins, in a self-pitying but also self-destructive fantasy. The familiar's identity is ambiguous, but in the sense that the writer is an enchanter, as source of his power the familiar may be his own imagination. As the imagination becomes a defamiliarized Other it produces a plot of destruction and torment.

Because the rescue justifies aggressive action, its violence is frequently ignored. Focus on the maiden's plight and the hero's rescue denies the prior fantasy of torment. The Andromeda myth conforms to the paradigm; its myth of rescue conceals aggressive and possessive themes with a veneer of charity.

Many other Victorian rescue scenes suggest a similar subtext, one different from heroism. The rescue in John Everett Millais' *The Knight Errant* (1870, figure 1.2), for example, presents a scene containing the possibility of rape as well as rescue.[13] The painting resembles others of the period in which a knight rescues a woman from a sexual assault.[14] Millais' painting shows the knight cutting the bonds of a naked woman who has been attacked and mistreated by a knight whose slain body lies in the upper right background. Bits of the woman's clothes appear scattered at her feet. Wisps of hair blow across her hip and thigh. The woman averts her head from the knight and from the viewer, a revision Millais made when it was thought that the lady's direct gaze out of the canvas made her appear shameless.[15]

The painting focuses on the bound nude whose rope-bitten flesh shines. At her feet a rumpled or torn piece of clothing picks up her skin tones as does the crescent moon in the upper left background. The knight rescues the lady from a fastidious distance, cutting her bond with his sword, the tip of which is blood-stained. In contrast to the knight's metallic containment, the woman is messy, her body generous. The symbolism of the prominently displayed instrument of liberation contributes to the painting's sexual innuendo, not only alluding to the slaying of the wicked knight but also suggesting the woman's defloration. The broken moon adds to the symbolism of violated chastity. The knight rescues a woman presented as an erotic object, helpless and exposed, but with a body charged with potentially dangerous energy. He frees the woman but with caution.

Millais' rescue scene, as a fantasy, is susceptible to oedipal interpretation. The knight, errant like Oedipus, wanders in the

1.2. John Everett Millais, *The Knight Errant*
Reproduced by the permission of the Tate Gallery, London.

light of the moon into a situation where a man assaults a naked woman, a symbolic analogue to what Freud calls the "primal scene." He slays the assailant and frees the woman, showing his fear of the fallen woman by hiding from her. Clad in grayish armor resembling in texture and tint the birch bark of the tree, the knight appears camouflaged in a forest of silvery browns and greens. Does he hide from the danger of her body, as though she threatened him like Medusa? Or does his distancing of himself from the woman underline his praiseworthy self-control? This knight may also be understood as having killed his own more aggressive self, represented in the slain knight, his mirror image, who has been punished presumably for failure of sexual restraint.

The many interpretative possibilities in Millais' painting call attention to psychological motifs implicit also in the story of Perseus and Andromeda. The Perseus myth, too, lends itself to an oedipal interpretation. Perseus begins his adventures in order to slay Medusa, an act that will rescue his mother Danaë from a plotting king. As a knight errant, his rescuing ways continue when he encounters Andromeda, saves her from a sea monster, and impregnates her with a son. Considering rescue fantasies a form of "male love," Freud claims that they are associated with giving birth, especially when they are found in connection with water: "A man rescuing a woman from the water in a dream means that he makes her a mother which . . . amounts to making her his own mother."[16] The fantasy expresses the boy's gratitude to his mother for giving him life by rescuing her from a peril and giving her a son, a replacement for himself. Like the oedipal rescuer, Perseus makes Andromeda (whom he first sees at the water's edge) a mother, conflating the purpose of his quest to free his mother with the goal of finding a wife. Thus, the hero wins his oedipal battle. Freud's interpretation accords with a familar Victorian domestic myth and in many respects derives from those values.

In addition to ignoring the possible titillation of fantasizing about women's suffering, to consider only the heroism of rescue as a form of male love mutes the proprietary nature of that particular conception of love. The form of love figured as rescue in the Andromeda myth ends in legal and sacred possession of the woman. This less romantic motive hides under the label "love." The only

Victorian painter to depict the moment of Andromeda's rescue imagined the rescuer not only as Millais' nocturnal knight errant but also as a fortune hunter. William Gale (1823–1909) rates barely a footnote in the canon of Victorian art, but he distinguished himself as a Royal Academy student by winning a silver medal in 1844. In 1851, 1852, and 1856, he exhibited Andromeda paintings at the British Institution and the Royal Academy. In the foreground of *Perseus and Andromeda* (1856?, figure 1.3) the newly slain dragon is draped over a rock, deflated as well as killed. The maiden has been shackled with her hands uplifted, her position exhibiting to advantage her graceful form. Her long hair wafts over her midriff from ribs to pubis, covering but suggestive of what is covered. Her head and eyes are cast down, but it is not clear whether her position denotes modesty or coyness in relation to her liberator. Perseus braces himself on Andromeda's rock while he hacks off the maiden's handcuffs. Pegasus rears his head in the background. The hero is dressed as a Roman warrior, and the allusion to Ovid in the catalogue, "Then seized the prize of his victorious fight, Andromeda," notes the influence of the Latin poet on the painter's interpretation.

As Ovid tells the story, Perseus does not instinctively spring to the rescue, but, after observing the advancing monster and hearing Andromeda's screams, he first approaches her lamenting parents, recites his former deeds, and strikes a bargain:

> If I were to ask for this girl's hand, I ought surely to be preferred to all other suitors as a son-in-law: but I shall try to add a further service to my present claims, if only the gods are on my side. I make this contract with you, that she shall be mine, if my valour can save her.[17]

Gale's Andromeda assumes the status of a valuable material prize, an exchange in the male commerce in women, and a token of appreciation. The reward for valor, she seems almost as limp as the poor crocodile-shaped monster. Occupying the center of the painting, her skin the lightest tone, Andromeda's body advertises itself as much a trophy as the dead beast. In the background Pegasus dramatizes the excitement that the erotic treasure promises. Since the flying horse arose from the Medusa's blood, Pegasus

(20)

also comprises booty for a monster slain. Unlike the formidable body of Millais' beauty, Gale's Andromeda poses like a pretty toy. Around her Gale arranges Perseus' other rewards: serpent skin, winged horse, and shield. In Gale's representation, rescue is a business arrangement, with a contract. Like a soldier of fortune, the hero takes his valuables.

In addition to expressing the rescuer's own need to be saved and his empire-building aspirations, interpretations of the myth could also separate active and passive aspects of masculinity. As an archetypal Victorian man, Perseus works at being a hero, driven by forces out of his control to perform great deeds. But men of less vigorous temperament might experience such an ideal as burdensome, threatening, and even tedious.[18] Certain male artists, ambivalent about conventional masculine and feminine stereotypes, used the figure of a passive woman to represent that aspect of themselves which the culture increasingly denoted as feminine. Robert Browning among the poets, for instance, imagined himself as the chained and helpless Andromeda. The myth of masculinity as valiant Perseus mirrors an image of man as passive "feminine" Andromeda.

The rescue of a maiden was a way to portray the ambiguous and conflicted identity of the hero. George Eliot, who does not write explicitly about Perseus but is the only woman writer to follow the myth's paradigm, explores the problem of using rescue as an external way of resolving personal uncertainties. *Daniel Deronda,* taking a cue from *Frankenstein,* could be aptly subtitled "The Modern Perseus." Like Shelley, Eliot gives us a wise and restrained perspective on male heroic fantasies, showing male need and vulnerability impelling the male starring role. The ending to *Daniel Deronda* demonstrates how rescue establishes firm gender definition as a way of confirming social identity. By focusing on rescue as a problem, Eliot questions both gender divisions and definitions of heroes and heroines.

Eliot's first scene shows her at work complicating the terms of the melodramatic story as she presents Gwendolyn Harleth as a

1.3. William Gale, *Perseus and Andromeda*
Courtesy of the Paul Mellon Center for Studies in British Art.

creature akin more to a Medusa than to an Andromeda. Daniel disarms her by fixing an "evil eye" on the gambling Gwendolyn, taking away the mysterious power of the "serpentine woman," whose good luck immediately turns to bad. Eliot reinforces the association of Gwendolyn with snakes by referring to her first as a Nereid (one of the jealous creatures causing Andromeda's doom) who has "got herself up as a sort of serpent." Observers note her "*ensemble du serpent*" and refer to her as a "Lamia beauty," objecting to "the revival of serpent worship." Daniel's redeeming of her necklace of turquoise stones "mortifies" her.[19] The episode reveals an assumed author playing with her Perseus' rescue fantasies, establishing Daniel, first as a would-be rescuer, then as an actual rescuer of Mirah, finally as a would-be "Deliverer" of his people (Book 7, ch. 51).

Eliot shows that the hero's rescuing is tied not only to a strong sense of duty but to ignorance of his true identity. Daniel's indecision about his vocation and the mystery of his parentage leads him to the symbolic action of rowing up and down the Thames. Drifting aimlessly on the river, he spies a maiden in great emotional distress. In a contemplative mood he sings a fragment of a Rossini aria which, echoing across the water, meets a responsive ear in the suicidal maiden: "Nella miseria." After Deronda saves the woman from her inner despair and the drowning river currents, Eliot comments:

> Deronda felt himself growing older this evening and entering on a new phase in finding a life to which his own had come—perhaps as a rescue; but how to make sure that snatching from death was rescue? The moment of finding a fellow-creature is often as full of mingled doubt and exultation as the moment of finding an idea. (Book 2, chap. 17)

Eliot makes overt and explicit the element of uncertainty which lies beneath many other Victorian treatments of the rescue myth. She questions the responsibility of the rescuer for the rescued—a question resolved in the myth and novel alike by the marriage plot. And she understands that the act of rescuing may save the hero in various ways but most centrally by solidifying his identity. The rescuer now has found an external goad to action which fulfills his heroic potential, but he has also expressed his own vulnerability by identifying with the despondent maiden.

The helpless maiden's plight mirrors Daniel's confused identity, only one sign of which is his hidden Jewishness. Not only are Mirah and Daniel marginalized and without knowledge of their mothers, but the gender of the hero is also questionable. Overtly, of course, he is male. The language of heroines, however, infuses Eliot's description of a soft, lovely creature whose clothes enhance his attractiveness. Furthermore, like many heroines of Victorian novels, Daniel plays a moral role. Like Agnes in *David Copperfield* he leads upward those whose lives touch his. Like many women, too, Daniel feels the demands of others as commands to subordinate himself to their wishes, to submerge his own desire so as to conform with those whose needs he feels as compelling. In Eliot's fable the Jew and the woman are combined in their marginality and become absorbed in Daniel's persona. As Michael Wolff argues, the implicit "otherness" of women, mirrored in the otherness of the Jew, is figured in Daniel not only as Jew but also Daniel as woman.[20]

The marriage between Mirah and Daniel signifies the unifying of identity. No longer drifting, Daniel finds an external mission which expands on his inner conflicts, projecting it on to the world of his people, the Jews. He combines the attributes of Perseus—he wishes to rescue his people from dispersal and possible annihilation by founding a nation—and of Andromeda—he is vulnerable, marginal, and from a dark race.

Eliot's episode draws much of its appeal from elements in a quintessentially Victorian configuration of the Andromeda myth—rescue measuring heroic character—for the rescuer must respond to the exigency at hand with only his moral fiber as preparation. But Daniel, like the nameless hero in Millais' picture, is a knight errant with his own complex reasons for being a rescuer. Eliot questions the problematic nature of rescue in various ways before she allows the most successful rescue, as in the myth, to culminate in marriage. She traces Daniel's increasingly less successful efforts to save Gwendolyn Harleth and his own mother, who, like Perseus' mother, is a princess. Unlike Danaë or Andromeda, the Princess Halm-Eberstein frees herself from "the bondage" (Book

7, ch. 51) of being a Jew, and with more awareness than the mythological princesses, blames her father, accusing him of "fettering me into obedience" (Book 7, ch. 51). With Mirah and Daniel's marriage, the couple disappear into an idealistic and questionably successful mission, to be a Deliverer, as his grandfather had wished. Unlike the myth, the couple's dynastic fate is left uncertain. They probably will not found a race, name a kingdom. From the point of view of the rescuer, suggests Eliot, saving someone creates heroic conflicts not entirely resolved by becoming a savior.

The Politics of Bondage: Andromeda

IF ONE looks under the entry "Andromeda" in *The Oxford Companion to Classical Literature,* one is given the terse command: "See Perseus." As if somehow incidental to Perseus' story, the maiden is an auxiliary, not doing anything in her own right. An object for someone else's heroic rescue, she is doomed without even the dignity of having her fate a consequence of her own actions. Casseopeia, her mother, was being punished through her for bragging too extravagantly about mortal beauty, thus enraging the Nereids. With nothing but her hair waving in the wind to distinguish her from the inanimate rocks, Andromeda apparently deserves no special reference of her own.

Victorian versions of the Andromeda myth deny this erasure, emphasizing the maiden in her passive role. Nina Auerbach, in *Woman and the Demon,* demonstrates how fear of vital female energy dominates a significant version of Victorian mythmaking. Although ultimately domesticated and not overtly demonical, Andromeda exercises greatly imaginative power. In spite of her apparent role as merely the product of a male story, a story of the birth of his heroism rather than of her threatened martydom, Andromeda's very silence is insisted upon as a subject. From that perspective, the characterization of the bound maiden actively testifies to her creation as a particular kind, and a prescriptive kind, of woman. The other side of the demonic coin, her domestication responds to the barbarism of her opposite. The fact of her importance is noted in the final sentence of the Oxford's Perseus entry: "The legend of Perseus and Andromeda is the subject of a poem by C. Kingsley, 'Andromeda.'"

Andromeda's plight was powerful in itself, without reference to Perseus. For some, her name alone alluded to a genre of representations in which passivity allied with martyrdom to suggest pornographic victimization.[21] In comparing the moral climate of England in 1876 to that of "falling Rome," John Ruskin castigated the exploitation of suffering nudes as subjects for titillating pictures. In Gustave Doré's Bond Street gallery: "You have a picture of highly dressed harlots gambling, of naked ones, called Andromeda and Francesca of Rimini, and of Christ led to be crucified . . . "[22] Andromeda as a label for a type signifies a range of debased representation, derived from interpreting nude figures in relation to each other. Doré's illustration of Ariosto's *Orlando Furioso,* in which the incident of Angelica's rescue is adapted from Ovid, torment combines with an artistic pose, giving a new meaning to the concept of the "pin-up" (figure 1.4). The woman appears to hang in chains, revealing sinuous curves, echoed in monster, waves, and rocks. Ruskin's critique of such works places Andromeda in relation to both the damned Francesca and the martyred Christ. Doré's iconography, claims Ruskin, connects nude harlots to the nude Christ and signifies a fallen London. The interest in tortured bodies divested of moral and spiritual meaning profanes the most sacred subject and perverts the meaning of Andromeda's travail as it blasphemes Christ's sacrifice.

Without directly addressing the question of pornography, Ruskin alludes to it. Recent analyses of European pornographic images of women in *fin de siècle* and surrealist art provide some models for examining earlier works, such as Victorian Andromeda paintings. Bram Dijkstra's *Idols of Perversity: Fantasies of Feminine Evil in Fin-de-Siècle Culture* argues that the representations of women at the turn of the century reveal a deeply misogynistic culture. Further, he argues that the same misogyny is connected to anti-Semitic and racist theories of the twentieth century. Aryan theories of racial supremacy also can be found in Victorian times. Charles Kingsley and Frederic Leighton, for example, connect the Andromeda myth to ideas of racial supremacy, both accepting the opinion that Greek culture originated in a superior type of Aryan race. Perseus, an enlightened male, brings civilization to Andromeda, a barbarian princess. Racial and sexual supremacy coexist. Nakedness, chains, monster, and even marriage in this context are forms of domination. Unlike the female images in Dijkstra's study, English Victorian representations of the Andromeda myth domesticate perversity, deflecting that element with a conventional fairy-tale ending.

First chaining the maiden, the Andromeda myth then replaces that raw bondage with the more benevolent bonds of matrimony. Although potentially both perverse and pornographic, the myth

1.4. Gustave Doré, "Ruggiero and Angelica," illustration from Ariosto, *Orlando Furioso*
Reproduced with permission of Sterling Memorial Library, Yale University.

mutes those elements by its overt sympathy for the maiden's plight, its emphasis upon rescue rather than rape, and its morally correct ending. Were she not rescued, Andromeda would be eaten. Gustave Doré, in another illustration of *Orlando Furioso,* depicts the perverse image, imagined but rarely portrayed, of the beautiful naked woman as a piece of food (figure 1.5). The woman, a limp and sinuous fish in the dragon's maw, neither struggles not bleeds, her face frozen in an impassive but possibly ecstatic expression. The woman as a mouthful is not quite a martyr, but, if juxtaposed with Christ, Doré's picture might well cast an aura of unseemly sexuality on pictures of the Savior.

1.5. Gustave Doré, illustration from Ariosto, *Orlando Furioso*
Reproduced with permission of Sterling Memorial Library, Yale University.

To notice the similarity between such extreme images and more genteel ones points to the pornographic element in high art as well as the more sensational Bond Street offerings.[23] Images of naked women in chains stock the pornographer's repertory, but this image gains respect without losing its perverse eroticism when transformed into high art. The Royal Academy might confer respectability on some Andromeda paintings which nonetheless exploit an effect similar to Doré's more explicit pictures.

The same year that Millais showed *The Knight Errant,* Edward Poynter, R. A. President from 1896 to 1918, exhibited a small *Andromeda* (figure 1.6). Poynter's *Andromeda* is not about rescue but about bondage. His painting abstracts the chained maiden from the narrative, leaving her to stand as a martyr, comparable to Christ. The small painting employs a set of conventions about other chained maidens, combining exhibitionism with modesty, erotic pleasure with torment. An extravagant Mannerist drape swirls into the air and twines around the maiden's ankle, emphasizing rather than hiding or even masking her requisite nakedness. Her arms, chained behind her, enhance the fact of her naked body. As in Millais' picture, the woman averts her head as if in shame for her own exposed condition. Although her downcast eyes signify modest awareness of herself as open to intimate scrutiny, her opened lips are a Victorian sign of erotic pleasure. Like the drape, the whole of nature—waves, rocks, sky, and birds—swoons and swirls around her. Albeit unwillingly, she offers her body to the viewer's gaze, her mouth indicating that she is partly aware of her allure.

Female beauty, like the beauty of nature as Poynter imagines it, is patterned and potentially dangerous, reason in itself for chains. The wildly blown drape blends with the shape of the rocks to create a niche for the figure, and, echoing the pattern of waves, also makes visible a turbulent wind. Air, wind, waves, and the sinuous figure of the maiden are identified with one another. In spite of her shackles, which, with the drapery, are the signs of civilization, the woman herself is identified with what is outside culture, a wild, uncontrollable, natural beauty.[24] Her bonds control her danger and, further, make her a candidate for rescue.

Placed in a fabricated niche, the woman is taken from nature, civilized, and made into an icon. Poynter's representation shows

1.6. Edward Poynter, *Andromeda*
Courtesy of the Maas Gallery, London.

nature being subdued into culture. Naked woman is both part of nature and an erotic object for (male) culture to observe. Controlled by chains, Poynter's *Andromeda* exemplifies the power of the image of the woman in the myth; with no Perseus in the painting, she appeals mutely to the viewer.[25] Her name alone labels her as a victim who needs rescue, thus disguising how the image of her bondage becomes aestheticized. By calling the painting *Andromeda,* Poynter suggests two points in the Victorian sexual ideology: woman needs chaining and she needs saving. The artist portrays subjugation of the eroticized female object, an object deriving pleasure from being dominated.

The Sexual Politics of Interpretation: The Monster

ANDROMEDA MEANS "ruler of men." Certainly the Victorian poets who wrote about her knew that. In "med" Medusa's name has the same root, but, unlike Andromeda, the Gorgon's fatal power is acknowledged, and her punishment is commensurate with that power. Mirror images of each other, one female is killed because of her power, the other has her power chained. Although culturally assimilated to Perseus' story, Andromeda leaves a marker, a sign of power in her name. As woman and ruler of men, her name sets forth gendered distinctions elaborated in the narrative.

In addition to fixing opposite kinds of behavior for the two genders, the passive feminine and the active masculine, the Andromeda myth offers a third alternative, a sex that is not one: the monster that Perseus slays. In describing Shakespeare's theory of mythology, René Girard, citing Lévi-Strauss' notion of "undifferentiated," claims that monsters function as "a kind of undifferentiation." Although Girard is not referring to gender, his formulation can usefully apply to the monster's function in the Andromeda myth as sexually undifferentiated, potentially representing the gender of both sexes. The monster's unspecified gender, sufficient in itself to make it monstrous, first opens to question the duality of the sex/gender system. In a symbolic act the male destroys the possibility of indeterminate gender, implicitly stabilizing the gender system according to his political project. In regard to social identity Girard states: "In myth, as well as in ritual, undifferentiation is the prelude, the means and the *sine qua non* of re-differentiation."[26] Perseus affirms male and female identity by killing off other possibilities. In a culture that constructed the two sexes as polar opposites the dragon is useful to represent the horror of undifferentiation itself. Victorians have to be one sex or the other, but monsters can be both or neither. The sexual multivalence of the monster sign can therefore be powerfully significant, even in a single representation. Slaying the monster is the prelude to Perseus' and Andromeda's redifferentiation. The death of the undifferentiated one reaffirms the gender system by conferring upon the two humans the identity of man and woman and the status of husband and wife.

The third term—the non-gender—in the Andromeda myth loosens momentarily the bonds of the Victorian gender system, freeing the imagination to explore a wider spectrum of sexual identities than the cultural system would normally allow. The monster occupies an important existential position. On the boundary between sea and land, both in and out of nature, both in and out of culture, god-sent but not godly, it exists as a symbolic borderland. It can thus introduce an instability to polarized gender opposites, opposites that social change potentially could disturb. If, however, the possibilities of other kinds of gender arrangements are abolished, here by the symbolic action of slaying, the poles, reasserted, stand out in shining and solitary relief. There seem to be no alternatives.[27] Perseus slaying the dragon rescues the culture from its own disquieting questions not only about the connections between "normal" sexuality and aggression but also about the inevitability of sexual difference itself.

The two monsters, the dragon and Medusa, allow for the defining of a binary gender system. They merge at times, are mirror images of each other and of the two human characters. One paradigm of the myth figures Perseus first slaying unrestrained female power, embodied in the Medusa's capacity to petrify men. She is so dangerous, so invincible, that her mere glance will vanquish any male, turning him to stone. But Andromeda herself could be regarded as the good sister of this monstrous female.[28] As a civilized version of the petrifying female, Andromeda can be domesticated into an acceptable wife, yet she bears traces of her threat in her name. By slaying the Medusa and freeing Andromeda, the hero tames the chaotic female, the very sign of nature, simultaneously choosing and constructing the socially defined and acceptable feminine behavior. He thus assures himself of licensed rather than unlicensed sexuality, legitimate progeny, and protection of his household name.

Perseus keeps the Medusa's head. Her serpentine hair, like that of the Lamia, represents her as having appropriated male activities. By killing her and keeping her head, Perseus reclaims whatever masculine power she had stolen. Similarly, the dragon is sexually threatening. It is about to devour the naked maiden in an obviously aggressive and violent act, frequently interpreted as sexual violence. The orality of monsters is often a female equivalent, its open mouth a symbolic counterpart to fantasies of devouring female genitals.[29] The sea monster's long tail can also function as a phallic symbol. With their amorphous genders, both dragon and Medusa can represent bestial aspects of sexual intercourse. The monster's aggression justifies Perseus' aggression against it, but its indeterminate sex also provides a variety of meanings to its being killed. When the narrative ends, the possibilities opened and explored are closed off, resolved. The eternally feminine marries the indisputably masculine, and they live happily ever after.

The couple emerges from a treacherous event into a recognizable, almost anticlimactic domesticity. The form of idealized domesticity seems preferable to the chaos and danger of the debased world preceding it. Monsters no longer thrive, given patriarchal control; the resolution in marriage reinforces a recognizably patriarchal form of power relations, yet one that respects the wife as a treasure. Property, nation, marriage provide attractive alternatives to pestilence, daughter sacrifice, primitive gods. As a sacred narrative, with a status above that of other kinds of plots, myth can justify social claims.[30] In that sense the Andromeda myth justifies Perseus' claim as a patriarch. The story presents the hero as earning his reward by his feats, recognized by the gods as a worthy person for divine aid. Some Victorians acknowledge the hero's dependence upon Athena, a goddess who characteristically identifies with male privilege. Thus, Victorian domesticity seems sanctified by the Andromeda myth, which claims a timeless inevitability for the institution of marriage, and within that institution, for specific appropriate gender behavior.[31]

With the exception of Eliot's allusions, no woman writer treats the Andromeda myth; apparently its patriarchal terms did not leave them the scope to conceive of womanly activity. If women writers who narrated a heroine's efforts to move from parents to a challenging place for adult energies and needs had told Andromeda's plight, they might have imagined other options for her. Charlotte Brontë, Elizabeth Barrett Browning, and George Eliot, to name only three prominent Victorian writers, imagined woman's passage from parents to husband as filled with prosaic risks and scanned the larger world where women might have a variety of different options. Andromeda's lack of choice is particularly relevant as fable for a vexed moment in the history of English gender construction, a moment of the sentimentalization of marriage when at the same time middle-class women began to imagine other choices. The Victorian remakings of the Andromeda myth function as a prescription, a conservative remedy for the disease of the times. The chained woman waiting to be rescued responds to the challenge of a new kind of woman who will claim that she can unshackle herself, once she can control reproduction, own property, and work outside the home. The myth counters feminist aspirations by telling the maiden that she needs the hero, she needs marriage. After the story renders the terrible danger of unmarried woman, it offers an ending apparently happy as well as inevitable. Andromeda must marry to promote national goals. She must behave in a prescribed way so that the myth can end in happy marriage and prosperous empire. Given Andromeda's alternatives, who would not choose marriage?

So represented, the Andromeda myth justifies lines of gendered authority potentially challenged by Queen Victoria. The danger of transgressing gender boundaries was a particularly noticeable issue during the reign of a mother-queen. With Victoria on the throne, the institution of monarchy was subject to a particular conflict of gender definition. Reassuringly, the royal couple fitted themselves into conventional domestic mythologies while manifestly challenging them. Particularly as it was publicly represented, their lives both established bourgeois habits and conformed to them. Like their mythic counterparts, Victoria and Albert enjoyed the connubial pleasures of dynastic bliss. The difference in power relations between them and the mythological couple is the difference that counts. Victoria was Queen, but Albert was not King, a significant difference which produced continuing conflicts about hierarchy. Theirs was a conflict of power endemic to a female married Queen who reigned in an age which insisted upon the subservience of the wife in regard to her husband and lord.

Victoria and Albert's familial focus resembles Perseus and Andromeda's domestic tranquillity and also expresses the conflict encoded in Andromeda's name. Symbolically the ruler of men, Victoria assimilated the irreconcilable roles of complaisant wife and ruling monarch to her regal identity. The particular contradiction between dominance and submission expressed itself in elaborate debates about ceremonial protocol and in an eighteen-year argument between Ministers, Parliament, and Her Royal Majesty about what to call the Queen's husband, Victoria preferring "King Consort." The decision was only rendered six years after the Great Exhibition when the first Royal Princess was married in 1857, representing in its solution the royal family's version of the Andromeda myth's significance. In a memo, written just before the decision in favor of Prince Consort, the Queen described her incongruous position:

> While the wife of a King has the highest rank and dignity in the realm after her husband assigned to her by law, the husband of a Queen regnant is entirely ignored by the law. This is the more extraordinary, as a husband has in this country such particular rights and such great power over his wife, and as the Queen is married just as any other woman is, and swears to obey her lord and master, as such, while by law he has no rank or defined position. This is a strange anomaly.[32]

In her confusions about who was ruler—Albert in the marriage, Victoria in the realm—the monarch dramatized the disturbing gender changes occurring on all levels of the culture to which we give her name.

As if to confirm the paradoxical relation between Her Royal

Majesty and the mythological ruler of men, Queen Victoria presented John Bell's monumental and sensuous *Andromeda* (figure 1.7) as a gift to her Consort. The Queen selected that particular statue from the thousands of choices available at the Great Exhibition of 1851. Solidly anchored in a garden designed by Albert at Osborne House in the Isle of Wight, Bell's *Andromeda* presents in its structure the ideological project I have been tracing. A large-framed Andromeda, whose bondage is prominently and suggestively displayed, stands on a symbolic pedestal, consisting of Medusa's head and four putti riding dolphins and brandishing knives. The chained victim's modestly lowered head reinforces one meaning of her chain as subjugation. To read figure and pedestal together suggests that the statue represents the self-effacing yet strong victim rising above the remains of her shameless, and therefore more monstrous, counterpart. Bell's *Andromeda* presents an ambiguous triumph of the wife over the monster but reminds the viewer of the force required for such a triumph. As representative of Victorian gender ideology, Andromeda served as a figure for many conflicts that were in part reflected by the couple who bought Bell's statue.

Many Victorians used the Andromeda myth to represent dramatically conflicts in the dominant gender system. Although myth claims a realm beyond the temporal, history produces it. Both descriptive and prescriptive, myth transforms history into nature, making what is provisional seem natural. Presented as a traditional sacred narrative, the myth allows no questioning of its eternal truth, the mythic realm denying the contingency of facts and time. When considered as motivated, however, with designs on a reader/spectator, representations of the Andromeda myth can be understood in political, contingent, contextual terms. My discussion of Victorian interpretations of the Andromeda myth assumes what my epigraph from Barthes asserts—that they are fabricated from cultural data. Representations of the Andromeda myth, taken together, essentialize the sexual politics of dominance and hierarchy while at the same time express conflicts over proper gender definitions of masculinity and feminity as such personal matters assimilate to cultural norms and institutions—church, marriage, science, law, art, and literature.

(36)

As the century was ending, the other side of the myth's potential meaning began to take over. Medusa and Andromeda began to change places, the monstrous woman standing above her domesticated counterpart. As Mark Girouard has shown, Victorian and Edwardian revivals of chivalry died with the First World War.[33] Moreover, with the agitation for female suffrage, marriage seemed a less definitive way to tame woman's dangerous power.

For a time during Victoria's reign, although its terms were contested by other myths and other kinds of representations, the Andromeda myth claims privilege and authority for men, opposing to those claims an acquiescent female, benevolently and legitimately subjugated by marriage. While social agitation, laws, and the Queen's ruling presence challenged that dichotomy, the myth seemed to float above politics in a realm of absolutes, assuring the embattled system of eternal verities, an assurance beyond the power even of established religion, itself suffering the blows of schism, scientific challenge, and new methods of biblical study. The Perseus and Andromeda myth becomes a counter-plot to the fantasies of woman's liberation. It too is a plot of liberation, but instead of transforming the House of Lords into the House of Lords and Ladies, or making the House of Commons safe for women, Andromeda is liberated into a common household. Victorian women's fictions expressed a growing desire for independence, property, education, and work, and represented the limitations of female roles in images of constriction and starvation.[34] At the same moment the middle-class Victorian males discussed in this book dreamed of chivalrous Perseus rescuing eternally grateful Andromeda.

1.7. John Bell, *Andromeda*
Reproduced with permission of Yale Center for British Art,
Paul Mellon Collection. From the Great Exhibition Catalogue.

CHAPTER TWO

Manly Allegories

H, MY dear man, the beauty of that whole myth is unfathomable," the Reverend Charles Kingsley wrote of the Andromeda myth to his fellow Christian Socialist J. M. Ludlow. Kinsley had spent months in 1852 pluming the depths of the myth's meaning before writing his longest, most ambitious poem, "Andromeda." "I love it, and revel in it more and more the longer I look at it."[1] Kingsley visualizes the myth's deep beauty to discover its mysterious, allegorical meaning. Although their derived meanings differ, the four men discussed in this chapter, William Etty, William Edward Frost, Charles Kingsley, and Gerard Manley Hopkins, interpret the myth allegorically. In addition, for these four men the woman in pain is a specific part of the story. To some extent they regard the nude woman's pain not so much with pity as with pleasure. Allegory permits, perhaps even promotes, this double vision—representing the highest human emotions and values while also representing bondage.

Abstracting meaning from representation, allegory separates the rational (or rationalized) meaning from the emotional depiction.[2] Andromeda may represent Faith assailed by Lewdness, or Woman rescued by Man from any number of Errors, interpretations used by Hopkins and Kingsley respectively. Or she may represent, more generally, Affliction, as she probably does in Etty and Frost's pictures. For Kingsley, Andromeda's rescue also represents Barbarism rescued by Civilization; for Hopkins, the Church rescued by Christ. Torment, thus, not only becomes spiritual, it can become religious.

To rationalize the maid's suffering distances pain from its concrete representation as a bound woman. Actual physical pain seems not an end but only the means of depicting in concrete terms the myth's allegorical, spiritual meaning. Kingsley, for example, in desiring to recreate a classical sensibility for his version of the Perseus and Andromeda myth, believed he was subordinating emotion to reason. Using as his model what he calls "objective classical poetry" (*LM* 2:83), he wished to make the myth speak for itself: "I want to aim at the clearest and sharpest objectivity, and even in the speeches of Perseus and Andromeda, the subjective element must come out in sententiousness, not in sentiment" (*LM* 2:85).

Even as he interpreted the myth allegorically as a paradigm of Victorian family life, Kingsley denied that he was writing allegory. Although he disavowed one kind of allegory as too dependent on arbitrary ciphers interpreted in ways unintended by the author,[3] he writes what Alastair Fowler describes as an allegorical genre—in this case an epic modulated by allegory.[4] Kingsley studied Homer's hexameters and the dramas of Sophocles "to catch the sententiosity" (*LM* 2:85). To achieve the authority of enduring wisdom, he tries to emulate the rationality his age thought of as classical.

The objectivity associated with sententiousness in literature also applies to the painter's valuation of history painting. Recording dramatic scenes from literature, mythology, and human events, history painting claims to present high moral and spiritual values objectively true as exemplified by events in legend and history. Although the high status of history painting was changing during the Victorian period,[5] Etty and Frost subscribed to the definition given by Royal Academy President John Opie in 1809:

> The empire of the art [of history painting] extends over all space and time: it brings into view the heroes, sages, and beauties of the earliest periods, the inhabitants of the most distant regions, and fixes and perpetuates the forms of those of the present day; it presents to us the heroic deeds, the remarkable events, and the interesting examples of piety, patriotism, and humanity of all ages and, according to the nature of the action depicted, fills us with innocent pleasure, excites our abhorrence of crimes, moves us to pity, or inspires us with elevated sentiments.[6]

Opie's metaphor of empire suggests the canon-making mission of history painting, fixing and perpetuating values by colonizing the past. Artists gained in stature by presenting mythological scenes as having an allegorical meaning, although that meaning was not always specified. By calling the gazer's pleasure "innocent," Opie answers possible objections to some subjects, casting the elevating light of the historical genre on, for example, chained naked women, called Andromeda.[7] In Opie's words, history painting's subjects are "interesting examples of piety, patriotism, and humanity." Allegorized to personify noble ideas, they provide *exempla* for moral improvement. Making history painting's canon thus involves a process of interpretation, similar to the allegorizations whereby classical history and mythology were made compatible with Christian doctrine.[8]

Some writers on allegory distinguish between literary and pictorial allegories, calling allegorical figures in paintings merely "personifications."[9] What is important here, however, is not the differences between pictorial and literary allegory but their similar principle of presenting an embodied abstract meaning. Personification characteristically clothes abstractions in a female body, adding concrete objects, such as chains, to symbolize attributes. Like literary allegory, personification dissociates representation and interpretation. The figure of Andromeda as a personification can be easily assimilable to traditions of allegorical representation. Once made abstract, Andromeda's bondage can be exalted or rationalized. Allegorical representations of the myth construct gender by deploying sexual differences according to male dominance and female submission, given an abstract meaning.

"Great Actions and the Human Form": Etty and Frost

WILLIAM ETTY dedicated himself to painting nude women, the first English painter to so specialize.[10] Although reviewers found many of his paintings lacking in refinement and taste, there is no evidence that Etty himself was aware of a pornographic element in his work, an element not discountable by considering his contemporary viewers as prudish. With consistent earnestness he cited his paintings as chaste studies of great themes and pleasing forms. Professional reasons determined his selection of Andromeda for the subject of at least four canvases, two of Perseus rescuing Andromeda and two of Andromeda alone, one a full-figure study of the woman, and one of Andromeda's upper body.

Etty explained in his diary his development from a painter of natural phenomena to a history painter. At first he found the sky and the effects of light and clouds an inspiration but then discovered that tradition valued other subjects more highly: "Afterwards, when I found that all the great painters of Antiquity had become thus great through painting Great Actions, and the Human Form, I resolved to paint nothing else."[11] When attacked for the voluptuousness of his nudes, Etty disavowed the manifest subject matter by recourse to the allegorical importance of history painting. Of his *Judith,* for example, he explains that as in all his pictures he has aimed "to paint some great moral on the heart:—Patriotism and Self-Devotion . . . to her country, her people, and her God."[12]

Etty's piety and dedication seem at variance with the blunt physicality of many nude images. The literalness of his rendition of nude figures combines with incongruous positioning, not simply awkward but discontinuous. Etty himself declared that he aimed for artlessness, for characters taken up by their situations as if they were performing the action regardless of aesthetic considerations, but most of his paintings seem studio poses, appearing to contemporary reviewers as appealing to degraded tastes. Defending himself against charges of impurity by dedicating his life to Art and echoing his explanation of Judith's heroic meaning, Etty vowed at the age of fifty-five not to marry, the vow not the less fervent for there being no prospects to tempt him: "Being in sound Mind and Body I declare it to be my firm intention NEVER TO MARRY. In which resolution I pray God to help me that I may devote myself more purely to my Art, my Country and my God!"[13] The concept of purity is used both by Etty's attackers and his defenders. Both share a notion that the separation of image and actuality would cleanse the vocation of sexual exploitation.

Etty himself disavowed any interest in his subjects as actual naked women. They were forms depicted for intrinsic beauty of shape and color. Following a common neoclassical practice, he used a kind of aesthetic cannibalization, frequently painting a pleasing part of one model combined with attractive parts of others.[14] Etty explained in his diaries the rational process whereby he came to an aesthetic appreciation of nude paintings. He first began to understand that they were the highest form of painting and later realized that of all human forms the female was the most highly prized:

> And finding God's most glorious work to be WOMAN, that all human beauty had been concentrated in her, I resolved to dedicate myself to painting—not the Draper's or Milliner's work,—but God's most glorious work, more finely than ever had been done.[15]

Etty presents the case for painting nudes as a gradual, rational, and educative process. He defers to the Almighty, claiming that representations of nude women are a form of praise to God. Although his nudes were influenced by Rubens' fleshly bodies and the highly colored Venetian paintings he admired, he himself separated his rational practice from sensuous effects. If one aspires to greatness, Etty claims, one paints the greatest subject. In painting nudes artists emulate the Almighty; nude paintings are therefore an artist's way of praising the Lord.

Gilchrist's defense of Etty's nudes responds to condemnation in reviews which described the paintings as impure, that is, merely carnal:[16]

> Admiration of Woman's form amounted in Etty to devotion. Belief in the purity of the nude when rendered in purity of heart, as in his own case, . . . was a religion with him: a religion innocent and true . . . Here all is consecrated to art—an expression of his,—might fittingly have been inscribed over Etty's studio.
>
> It was, in fact, the very purity of his life . . . and of his thoughts, the simplicity of his character, and the singleness of his aims, which enabled him to paint with a more fervid gusto of those beauties, than men of less intrinsic purity of character dare. "People may think me lascivious," Etty would protest: "but I have never painted with a lascivious motive."[17]

Sacramental language splits pure motives from fervid results. According to his defender and to Etty himself, the lack of conscious lascivious motive consecrates his art. The process of composition in which the figures are not actually modeled after one woman but are reconstituted wholes from various parts could disguise from the painter a voluptuous product. In the very process of painting, Etty dissociates his aesthetic concern with form from the effect of his rendering of nude subjects. The tension between voluptuousness of the paintings and his objective study and restudy of bodily forms contributes to the disjunctive quality in many Etty paintings.

The awkward composition of Etty's *Andromeda—Perseus Coming to Her Rescue* (1840, figure 2.1) results from the dissociation of the figures. The three figures, dragon, maiden, and Perseus riding Pegasus, bear little relation to each other. All three face the same way. Tracing its technique to Rubens, Dennis Farr finds in the picture: "a certain crudeness in the conception of the subject, particularly the unpleasant effect produced by the contorted pose of Andromeda."[18] Not only contorted, the maiden's figure lacks dramatic connection to the rest of the composition, dominating the picture both in her size and in the echoing of her pose by the other figures, particularly by the monster. Rather than appearing as the monumental maiden's mortal enemy, the sea serpent par-

2.1. William Etty, *Andromeda—Perseus Coming to Her Rescue*
Reproduced with permission of the Royal Albert Memorial Museum, Exeter.

odies her. Its eyes, like hers, look heavenward and not, as one might expect, at its prey. Its mouth with its fangs and lolling tongue parodies her open mouth. So positioned, with its undulating body a curvaceous echo of the maiden, the monster presents a debased, miniature counterpart of Andromeda. Perseus rides outward, not toward the other two figures, misdirecting his course past the objects of his mission.

Even when Etty painted a single figure, his composition can show a disconcerting lack of coherence. The most intimate, powerful, and pornographic of Etty's Andromeda paintings shows only a portion of the chained woman (figure 2.2). Like the rescue scene, the single figure is disconnected in its parts. Etty presents the upper third of Andromeda, conveying in her facial expression in intense emotion and the desperate situation of his subject, while the rest of the painting gives another, almost contradictory meaning to the expression. The painting combines eroticism with torment, producing a pornographic image.

Andromeda's attitude resembles many depictions of martyrs, where the tortured dévot implores heaven by looking upward. Andromeda's eyeballs turn to the heavens, in a facial attitude similar to his devout *Judith*. By winding Andromeda's chains under her breasts and rolling the eyeballs upward, Etty suggests the maiden's bodily torment. The pose recalls Renaissance and Baroque depictions of martyrdom, the eyes seeking deliverance from a higher authority. Revealing the Venetian influence, Andromeda's pose, with her eyes looking upward and her mouth slightly open, resembles Titian's depiction of the Virgin in his *Assumption* (1516–18). Moreover, in Ripa's iconographic handbook, Affliction is personified as a woman seated on a rock, her eyes cast upward.[19] Etty's Andromeda paintings employ the vocabulary of facial expression to suggest the maiden's travail. Iconographic allusions to religion augment rather than soften the pornographic effect.

The holiness of martyrdom expressed in Andromeda's face conflicts with the fleshly exactitude by which Etty renders her breasts, adding sensuous overtones to heavenly supplication. Andromeda's full breasts—round, with pointed nipples—dominate the painting. Dark shadows underneath emphasize their fullness. The left breast in the extreme foreground seems to offer

2.2. William Etty, *Andromeda*
Reproduced with permission of National Museums and Galleries on Merseywide.

itself to the viewer, while the right one highlighted both by shadows and by the lighted tip, extends into the painting's dark background. Chains wind beneath the breasts, a lock of hair rests above them, and a tendril points to each one.

Etty's perspective contributes to the pornographic effect, creating the illusion that the painter sits below the woman, possibly on her lap, looking up at her breasts. Since there is no other reference in the picture, the intensity of this close-up reinforces that impression. Discussing Victorian pornography, Steven Marcus describes the pornographer's mentality in terms that apply to Etty's *Andromeda:* "Inside of every pornographer there is an infant screaming for a breast from which he has been torn."[20] Both Marcus and Robert Stoller describe the revenge motive of pornography, in Marcus the specifically infantile rage at being deprived from the bliss of having the breast and at the futile effort to recapture it.[21] Etty's *Andromeda* lovingly represents the lost breast in conjunction with the feelings of revenge at its loss. The chains wound around the breasts and the woman's travail figure that revenge. Etty's *Andromeda* depicts sexual victimization as recapturing the breast and punishing its owner by chaining her.

So disconnected are the three separate elements in *Perseus and Andromeda* (after 1840, figure 2.3) that they seem parts of different paintings. Holding Medusa's head above his own, Perseus hangs in the air, held aloft by Mercury's winged slippers. He looks down at a Rubensian group of cavorting Nereids who seem to look up at him. The dragon-monster turns away from his prey, and, looking upward at the Medusa's head, is apparently in the process of being turned to stone. Andromeda stands in the foreground of the painting, chained to a rock with her hands upward. The drapery behind her enhances her form but also serves to create an illusion that she occupies a more secluded, almost inner, space. The drapery, falling on the monster's rear torso, renders that part of his body as a stationary object, like a chair or divan. Andromeda's exaggerated classical attitude, with its long curve from arm to knee, lends her a repose, as if she were stretching her arms upon awakening rather than being forced by fetters to assume an exposed grace.

William Edward Frost (1810–1877), a painter of nudes like his mentor, both imitated Etty's pornographic poses and made them prettier. Etty's influence over Frost began when the young painter was a youth of fifteen; so closely did the pupil imitate the master's style that their paintings are frequently hard to distinguish. Al-

2.3. William Etty, *Perseus and Andromeda*
Reproduced with permission of Manchester City Art Gallery.

though he was compared to Etty from the beginning, Victorian eyes found Frost's paintings more chaste than Etty's, the nudes less fleshly. The language of moral purity defends his paintings by seeking to remove Frost's pallid nymphs from the realm of carnality:

> Although Frost has followed Etty in some degree in choice of subject, in mode of colouring, and style of composition, he certainly cannot be regarded as his imitator, for he differs materially from him in the chastely-correct and highly-finished manner in which he depicts the undraped nymphs in his pictures. They are always full of grace and refinement, of beauty and feminine simplicity; and there is nothing in his pictures which the most delicate and highly-cultivated taste could disapprove.[22]

By calling nude women "nymphs," the critic recognizes their nonhuman quality. Frost's pictures seem empty of specific reference, almost interchangeable, with the same kind of girls who, with their clothes on, graced Keepsake albums. The critic's use of the word "chaste" insists on the virtue of the painter's motive and the refinement of his potentially uncivilized subject matter.

Frost favored a composition of nymphs in the water, splashing about in various attitudes. His *Andromeda* (1853, figure 2.4) is typical of many of his other pictures, but its very blandness demonstrates how the painter deflects the cruelty he portrays by what looks like a merry scene of girls playing in the surf. Using a similar grouping of splashing sea creatures as in the background of Etty's picture, Frost makes that Rubensian composition the center of his painting. Andromeda suffers among a community of women, with one darker figure in the foreground, possibly a Triton, blowing a horn. Andromeda's rock sets her above her companions, but, like them, she strikes a graceful attitude, one slender arm placed behind her head, the bent left elbow compositionally balancing the right bent knee. She is apparently chained by one wrist, but the handcuff connected to the background chain seems like a piece of jewelry. One blond nymph wears a similar bracelet, but higher on her arm. Andromeda looks upward, her head and eyes in a pose similar to two of Etty's Andromedas, scanning the

2.4. William Edward Frost, *Andromeda*
Courtesy of Christie, Manson & Woods.

heavens, an allegory of Affliction, turned by Frost into distracted Pique.

Frost's scene illustrates Milton's lines from "Il Penseroso":

> Or that Starr'd *Ethiop* Queen that strove
> To set her beauty's praise above
> The Sea Nymphs, and their powers offended.
> (ll. 19–21)

In 1848 Queen Victoria bought Frost's *Euphrosyne,* also known as *L'Allegro.* Frost was encouraged in his illustration of Milton by that success to illustrate the companion poem.[23] Frost's justification from the myth for including his bevy of pretty sea-spirits is that they have brought upon Andromeda her travail. In jealousy they prevailed upon Poseidon to send the monster. Frost depicts the moment before the sea-beast arrives. The maidens cavort in the water, attending the mythological counterpart of an execution, enjoying Andromeda's torment. Andromeda's eyes cast upward separate her suppliance to higher powers from their communal enjoyment. An added taunt, their gay poses show pleasure at Andromeda's pain.

Spiritual Exercises: Kingsley and Hopkins

DESPITE OBVIOUS differences, there are strong affinities between the intense asceticism of Hopkins and the religious enthusiasm of Kingsley.[24] Writing to the Canon Richard Watson Dixon, Hopkins finds "Kingsley and the Broad Church School" bumptious and unmannerly: "There is a whole volume of Kingsley's essays which is all a kind of munch and a not standing of any blasted nonsense from cover to cover."[25] On his part, Kingsley was repelled by the celibate Roman Church path that Hopkins chose, considering belief in the Infallibility of the Church and the Immaculate Conception to be insane. To him celibacy was a sign of effeminacy.

Their poems on the Andromeda myth seem at first to illustrate their differences. Hopkins' poem is a Miltonic sonnet; Kingsley's, his longest, is a narrative, written in hexameters imitative of

Homer's epic meter. Nevertheless, both poems celebrate marriage as a sacrament safeguarding men's control over women. Allegorical interpretation makes the myth relevant to their times. Kingsley's Perseus and Andromeda are avatars of Victorian domesticity, while Hopkins' mythological figures represent the plight of the contemporary Church. Both poems defend Christian marriage, connecting it to manly virtue.[26] Using different forms of allegory, each poet constructs a Victorian myth of Christian manliness. As each poem in its different way shows, the two churchmen's concept of manliness requires conventional marriage.

Whereas both clergymen praised the beauties of both nature and the male physique as emanating from the Creator, their praise of womanly beauty is usually connected to her physical suffering. Kingsley's paean to nature resembles that of the poet of "Pied Beauty" and "Spring:"

> *Never lose an opportunity of seeing anything beautiful.* Beauty is God's handwriting—a wayside sacrament; welcome it in every fair face, every fair sky, every fair flower, and for it *Him,* the fountain of all loveliness, and drink it in, simply and earnestly, with all your eyes; it is a charmed draught, a cup of blessing. (*LM,* 1:177)

As their appreciation of nature blesses the Creator, so both claimed that masculine muscles similarly showed God's fashioning hand. Both men admired working men's physical prowess, what Hopkins called "Amansstrength."[27] "Oh, there was a butcher's nephew playing cricket at Bramshill last week whom I would have walked ten miles to see, in spite of the hideous English dress," Kingsley remarked as he fantasied about the lad's additional allure, "One looked forward with delight to what he would be 'in the resurrection'" (*LM* 2:84). Hopkins' "Harry Ploughman" catalogues the hefty man's "thew," the power of "His sinew-service," his articulated muscles, "the scooped flank; lank/Rope-over thigh; kneenave; and barrelled shank."[28] Like Kingsley Hopkins attributed England's martial failures to a debased stock: "When I see the fine and manly Norwegians that flock hither . . . and walk our streets it fills me with shame and wretchedness."[29] As an antidote to effeminacy he proposed a remedy that Kingsley would have understood: pupils should imitate the Irish and play "football and other games barefoot on grass."[30]

Hopkins defines manliness as active, exemplified in his repudiation of the tendency in Keats' verse to "abandoning" itself to an "unmanly and enervating luxury":

> Nevertheless I feel and see in him the beginnings of something opposite to this, of an interest in higher things and of powerful and active thought . . . His mind had . . . the distinctively masculine powers in abundance, his character the manly virtues, but while he gave himself up to dreaming and self indulgence of course they were in abeyance.[31]

Both Kingsley and Hopkins held before themselves the manly ideal of rationality and self-discipline.

The two clerics experienced a Victorian religious conversion based upon renunciation. Both Kingsley and Hopkins invented various kinds of mortifications exceeding conventional practices. Kingsley made literal a connection between physical exercise and spiritual health, a connection made figuratively in the *Spiritual Exercises of Saint Ignatius* where physical fitness is analogous to religious ritual:

> For just as taking a walk, journeying on foot, and running are bodily exercises, so we call Spiritual Exercises every way of preparing and disposing the soul to rid itself of all inordinate attachments, and, after their removal, of seeking and finding the will of God in the disposition of our life for the salvation of our soul.[32]

Like Hopkins, Kingsley favored renunciatory exercises to strengthen his moral fiber. The man who frequently derided belief in miracles, stigmata, celibacy, and the Virgin Birth was attracted to the Church of Rome:

> I once formed a strange project, I would have travelled to a monastery in France, gone barefoot to the chapel at matins (midnight) and there confessed every sin of my whole life be-

> fore the monks and offered my naked body to be scourged by them.[33]

Kingsley invented his own exercises to gain ecstatic visions:

> I went into the woods at night and lay naked upon thorns and when I came home my body was torn from head to foot. I never suffered so much. I began to understand Popish raptures and visions that night, and their connection to self-torture. I saw such glorious things. (#36, 1843, Chitty, 75)

Hopkin's poetry also expresses a self-torment that is a more orthodox version of Kingsley's. In "Spelt from Sibyl's Leaves," metaphors of torture describe the mind in conflict: "selfwrung, selfstrung, sheathe-and shelterless, thoughts against thoughts in groans grind" (97). His terrible sonnets present an anatomy of agony, documenting his own paralysis in images of sexual impotence: "Time's eunuch, and not breed one work that wakes" (74), or with more self-mockery:

> And I that die these deaths, that feed this flame,
> That . . . in smooth spoons spy life's masque mirrored:
> tame
> My tempests there, my fire and fever fussy.
>
> (75)

Although Jesuit retreats and spiritual exercises provided Hopkins with one way of experiencing spiritual purification, like Kingsley, he derived meaning from images of taming emotional tempests by punishment and martyrdom.

What in Etty are iconographic similarities between Christian martyr and pagan victim are more explicit in Kingsley and Hopkins. Their Andromeda poems gain resonance in the context of their other poems of martyred women. In addition to two poems on the martyrdom of St. Dorothea, Hopkins described a magnificently martyred nun in "Wreck of the Deutschland:" "a lioness . . . A prophetess . . . a virginal tongue" (28). Kingsley detailed the martyrdom of St. Elizabeth of Hungary in both word and picture. His "Saint Maura. A.D. 304," a dramatic monologue and his favorite poem, imagines the pregnant Saint hanging naked on a cross while she describes to her husband (also tied to a cross) the nature of her tortures. In the same year that he wrote "Andromeda," Hopkins began but never finished two poems about women martyrs. In "Margaret Clitheroe" (145) he emphasized by italics the pregnant martyr's agony: "*Pressed to death.*" Caradoc in "Saint Winefred's Well" (152) describes the beautiful descent of the Saint's head after he decapitated her:

> What have we seen? Her head, sheared from her shoulders,
>   fall,
> And lapped in shining hair, roll to the bank's edge; then
> Down the beetling banks, like water in waterfalls,
> It stooped and flashed and fell and ran like water away.

Because she is rescued from bodily violation, Andromeda is a tamer version of these tormented women, but she also represents a way that torture maintains a boundary between rationality and emotion, between manliness and effeminacy.[34]

Both men insisted that rationality was a manly quality. Kingsley imagined the split between intellect and feeling as gendered. "The woman's part should be to cultivate the affections and the imagination," he instructed his bride, "the man's the intellect of their common soul" (*LM*, 1:70). Hopkins denied an emotional reason for his conversion to the Church of Rome. It was a simple case of addition: "I can hardly believe anyone ever became a Catholic because two and two make four more fully than I have."[35] In this equation the feminine, particularly a woman in torment, represents strong emotions denied to rational men. The spiritual exercise required by manliness found its complementary expression in descriptions of martyred women and provide a context for considering allegorical interpretations of the Andromeda myth.

Kingsley's Allegory and Matronly Interpretation

KINGSLEY'S "ANDROMEDA" praises Victorian domesticity, the Christian Socialist's adaptation of chivalric code. A proponent of socially active religion, which he called "Christian manliness," Kingsley constructed a version of patriarchy which divided all institutions and activities according to gender. At the center of society, marriage serves male needs, with submissive wives providing husbands with practice in ruling.[36] Like most of his works, "Andromeda" is homiletic; it is a Christian allegory of marriage, a guide for the proper sexual and gender roles for men and women. With Athene's aid, Perseus rescues Andromeda to educate her into the proper role of wife and mother. Andromeda with her chains is therefore re-presented as Mrs. Perseus, with matrimonial obligations.

This allegorical meaning, not immediately clear to the poet, required excavation: "You know the Andromeda myth is a very deep one," Kingsley concluded after weeks of thought, eventually discerning in it a contemporary story. His modern Perseus liberates the lady into marriage and ideal motherhood, rewards for her enlightenment and sexual fulfillment. The allegory extols a civilization in which the couple work together for the benefit of state, family, and private property, simultaneously transforming lust into communion, the grip of passion into the ties that bind.

Andromeda arrives at her rewards because she is a good student. Kingsley's entire gender system is based upon pedagogy, seemingly initiated by a powerful female teacher but in fact mandated and orchestrated by a dominant man who requires that he seem dominated. To fit his project of cleansing the masses, Kingsley modified that part of the chivalric code in which a knight pledges himself to the service of a woman, proposing to middle-class women that they adopt the role of chatelaine: "There is latent chivalry, doubt it not, in the heart of every untutored clod," Kingsley assured the women at a lecture at the Working Men's College (*LM,* 2:200), urging them to transform those he liked to call the "Esaus" of England into the Christian men who do not live religion in the confines of a cloister but pray by farming and treating women properly and thus by fighting the battles of "Jesus Christ THE MAN" (15:267). His chivalric Christian system depends upon womanly power galvanized by his own vision. As he shows in "Andromeda," he discerned in the chained maiden a model for the ideal female protégée.

Conflicts between who is dominating and who is submitting

in Kingsley's gender system places the male deviser of this system in precarious control. A passage from Kingsley's first novel, *Yeast* (1848), encapsulates the paradox of the gendered conflict between dominance and submission: "He assumed no superiority. He demanded her assent to truths . . . " (15:124). The man apparently denies the hierarchy, which the next sentence asserts, by making the authoritarian system seem objectively true. The man does not acknowledge his own need as constitutive of that truth, but, taking the role of reason, he depends upon the woman's willingness to take the part of feeling. The narrator explains his hero's position in regard to the woman as absolute and unquestioning in her sphere of dominance, "on all points which touched the heart he looked up to her as infallible and inspired" (15:124). In his authoritarian system such concepts as infallibility and inspiration make questioning idle and submitting pleasurable.

The dominant man gently but firmly forces his beloved to rule him "in questions of morality, of taste, of feeling." Since he controls and wills his regression, submission to her guidance in those areas enables him to return, in an idealized form to his earliest relationship with his mother:

> . . . he listened not as a lover to his mistress, but rather as a baby to its mother; and thus, half unconsciously to himself, he taught her where her true kingdom lay,—that the heart and not the brain, enshrines the priceless pearl of womanhood, the oracular jewel, the "Urim and Thummim," before which gross man can only inquire and adore. (15:125).

Both baby and master, the gross man needs a willing female subject to be faceted and formed into an oracular jewel.

Perhaps because Kingsley requires a compliant subject, his notions of woman's education are frequently linked to a fantasy of bondage. Pedagogy not only includes the titilation of sexuality, but Andromeda's chains suggest to Kingsley a sexual bondage similar to his pornographic drawings. He had in fact failed in his attempts to illustrate the myth: "If I have made one drawing of Perseus and Andromeda I have made fifty, and burnt them all in disgust" (*LM*, 82), he wrote to Ludlow. Some of Kingsley's extant drawings, which combine torment with sexual activity, suggest the form of the destroyed ones. One shows Kingsley and his wife Fanny tied to a cross as they engage in sexual intercourse, and another depicts the couple being assumed to heaven in that same position and activity.[37] The vision of Andromeda's torment, stripped naked, appealed to him as a sign both of sexual servitude and of infantile and maternal union.[38]

Kingsley celebrates Woman's bondage as part of her beauty. To create civilization, what Kingsley calls in the poem "order and right," Andromeda attracts the man as an inanimate bound object. The hero transforms evil bondage to an uncivilized tribe and a perfidious mother to allegiance to him. First viewing Andromeda as an artifact, Perseus mistakes the living woman for "a snow-white cross on the dark-green walls of the sea-cliff" (16:185). As a symbol of woman's self-sacrifice, the cross transfers Christ's martyrdom to the woman. A Kingsley drawing portrays a naked woman with long black hair bent beneath a cross which she carries up a steep hill.

After his first sight of Andromeda as an attribute of herself in the cross, Perseus then sees her as a statue, an artifact. He explains to the distraught maiden that at first he thought she was not a real woman but a man-made representation:

> Carven in marble I deemed thee, a perfect work of the craftsman.
> Likeness of Amphitrite, or far-famed Queen Cythereia.
> (16:185)

In addition to characterizing Andromeda as a male creation, Perseus repeats the challenge to immortal beauty—comparing her beauty to Poseidon's wife, Amphitrite—which placed the maiden in jeopardy in the first place. Perseus identifies the cross, statue, and goddess as the threefold representation in "Andromeda" of the woman as wife.

An allegorical "drawing" in *Yeast* illustrates the importance of the threefold woman in Kingsley's patriarchy. *Yeast* is structured as an allegory of Christian manliness. The hero's name, Lancelot

Smith, suggests the polarities of the allegory: a chivalric Victorian knight from an honest workingman's background sets out to confront contemporary social issues that were fermenting like yeast. Although Lancelot feels the first glance between himself and Argemone Lavington as "eye-wedlock," the maiden contemplates a life of Christian asceticism and aspires to full English citizenship. Lancelot ingratiates himself into her household to convert her to an English maiden's true mission.

Lancelot draws allegorical pictures as a pedagogical aid, which Argemone finds "immaculate and inspired; for their chief, almost their only fault, was just those mere anatomical slips which a woman would hardly perceive" (15:125). "Triumph of Woman," a version of the Victorian tract on true womanhood, depicts woman's ethical sphere in relation to man:

> In the foreground, to the right and left, were scattered groups of men, in the dresses and insignia of every period and occupation. The distance showed, in a few bold outlines a dreary desert, broken by alpine ridges, and furrowed here and there by a wandering watercourse. Long shadows pointed to the half-risen sun, whose disc was climbing above the waste horizon. And in front of the sun, down the path of the morning beams, came Woman, clothed only in the armour of her own loveliness. Her bearing was stately, and yet modest; in her face pensive tenderness seemed wedded with earnest joy. In her right hand lay a cross, the emblem of self-sacrifice. Her path across the desert was marked by the flowers which sprang beneath her steps; the wild gazelle stept forward trustingly to lick her hand; a single wandering butterfly fluttered round her head. (15:128–129)

Like Andromeda, the allegorical Woman is naked, untouched by civilization but also uncivilized. This icon, described by Simone de Beauvoir, represents woman freed by various rituals from evil spirits: "She is the whole fauna, the whole flora of the earth," de Beauvoir describes the convention from which Kingsley draws: "gazelle and doe, lilies and roses, downy peach, perfumed berry, she is precious stones, nacre, agate, pearl, silk, the blue of the sky, the cool water of springs, air, flame, land and sea."[39] Woman mediates between man and Nature, her attributes the familiar symbols—cross, butterfly, and wild gazelle.

Although of nature, Woman's effect upon all civilized men is instantaneous and complete:

> As the group, one by one, caught sight of her, a human tenderness and intelligence seemed to light up every face. The scholar dropt his book, the miser his gold, the savage his weapons; even in the visage of the half-slumbering sot some nobler recollection seemed wistfully to struggle into life. The artist caught up his pencil, the poet his lyre, with eyes that beamed forth sudden inspiration. The sage, whose broad brow rose above the group like some torrent-furrowed Alp, scathed with all the temptations and all the sorrows of his race, watched with a thoughtful smile that preacher more mighty than himself. A youth decked out in the most fantastic fopperies of the middle age, stood with clasped hands and brimming eyes, as remorse and pleasure struggled in his face; and as he looked, the firece sensual features seemed to melt, and his flesh came again to him like the flesh of a little child. The slave forgot his fetters; little children clapped their hands; and the toil-worn, stunted savage woman sprang forward to kneel at her feet, and see herself transfigured in that new and divine ideal of her sex. (15:129)

Woman transfigures man, wordlessly conveying news from nature of what he has repressed to define civilization.[40] With the self-cancelling attributes of modesty and self-sacrifice, she is a knight of Christ, clothed in the "armour of her own loveliness."

Inspired by Woman, the aesthete experiences a religious conversion. The passage echoes Jesus' admonition in Matthew 18.4: "Verily I say unto you, Except ye be converted; and become as little children, ye shall not enter into the kingdom of heaven." Woman, the mighty preacher, requires no mediation of language, will, or intellect to perform her works. Though a degraded being, the fop converts because he actively knows himself as polluted in contrast to Woman's purity.

The "savage woman" acts as triumphant woman's foil. Like Woman, she has no prestige, no occupation, and no status, but unlike her, savage woman toils. Whereas Woman exists above culture as one pure and exalted, Female or "savage woman" exists below it as polluted and debased.[41] Woman shows to Female her ideal self.

Rather than interpret the drawing Kingsley requires that the male reader complete it: "to fill up the sketch himself . . . with the eye of faith." What needs to be filled is a void that the idealization of woman leaves in the culture. As the silence, the unvoiced, the repressed, Woman opens the way for male culture to inscribe its voice, a gap represented in the picture by gender asymmetry. Kingsley defines the men by their occupation: poet, scholar, artist, sage; or their status: sot, fop, slave, but Woman has neither occupation nor relationship. She is what Julia Kristeva describes as the semiotic, the receptacle through which structures articulate themselves.[42] The cipher, in anthropological terms, Woman is the base which supports the male prestige system,[43] seemingly at the top of the human hierarchy of values, but deriving her authority from the male will to power, masked as the will to be ruled.

"Triumph of Woman" is propaganda in the novel's sexual politics. Lancelot uses it to win Argemone for her dreams of celibate Christian devotion and feminism: "Ay! and to give up my will to any man!" Argemone exclaims, at the momet of her surrender: "to become the subject, the slave, of another human being! I, who have worshipped that belief in woman's independence, the hope of woman's enfranchisement, who have felt how glorious it is to live like the angels, single and self-sustained!" (15:134) Since the terms of debate offer Argemone only the choice between independent celibate or slave, given her passions, she has no viable choice. Viewing "The Triumph of Woman" converts Argemone to the dominant gender system, makes her willing to serve masculine creativity, to improve masculine character, and to marry.

Kingsley articulates connections between idealizations of women and masculine dominance. Argemone is "entranced with wonder and pleasure" at Lancelot's drawing, leading her both to adoration of its creator and to a new vision of her destiny:

> And her feelings for Lancelot amounted almost to worship, as she apprehended the harmonious unity of the manifold concep-

> tion . . . and when she fancied that she traced in those bland aquiline lineaments and in the crisp ringlets which floated like a cloud down to the knees of the figure, some traces of her own likeness, a dream of a new destiny flitted before her—she blushed to the very neck; and as she bent her face over the drawing and gazed, her whole soul seemed to rise into her eyes, and a single tear dropped upon the paper. (15:129)

By dominating the picture plane, the woman seems to command autonomous power, but that autonomy is delusional.[44] Triumphant Woman is not self-ruled but well-taught. "Woman will have guidance," the narrator asserts. "It is her delight and glory to be led; and if her husband or her parents will not meet the cravings of her intellect, she must go elsewhere to find a teacher" (15:130).

"Murder Will Out—and Love Too," the title of the chapter where "Triumph of Woman" persuades Argemone to renounce dreams of independence, indicates Kingsley's partial awareness of the violence required for the construction of his gender system. His illustration of the martydom of Queen Gertrude, mother of Saint Elizabeth of Hungary, reveals the subtext of his praise of woman.[45] He shows Gertrude's genitals being torched by a demon while other devils bite and pull at her naked body. Torture is the alternate controlling instrument to praise. As Lancelot drew "Triumph of Woman" to teach womanly submission, so Kingsley presented to his bride a life of the martyred Saint Elizabeth as a wedding gift, illustrated and written by him.

Like the Lancelot-Argemone episode in *Yeast,* "Andromeda" presents a woman being educated to her place in the world of civilized men. Andromeda's false notions do not compare to Argemone's aspirations to tread the "masculine ground of intellect" (15:22) but she also suffers from misconceptions about her true worth. Rescue delivers the maiden into the hands of a new servitude. Lecturing at the Working Men's College on "The Work of Ladies in the Country Parish," Kingsley offered "the true emancipation of woman" as an alternative to women who might be hoping for the vote and a career of their own:

> her emancipation, not from man (as some foolish persons fancy), but from the devil, "the slanderer and divider," who divides

> her from man, and makes her live a life-long tragedy . . . a life made up half of ill-usage, half of unnecessary self-willed martyrdom, instead of being, as God intended half of the human universe, a helpmeet for man, and the one bright spot which makes this world endurable. (*LM,* 2:200)

Man depends upon woman's dependency to make life endurable. Once she is educated Andromeda makes Perseus' world pleasant, safe, and prosperous.

"Andromeda" presents a woman before her triumph, like Argemone, learning how to become man's ideal being. As Kingsley imagined it, the myth shows a magnificent Greek boy bringing a higher vision of reality to a savage female. Before she is rescued, Andromeda's concept of divinity is primitive and dark. When adversity comes and she is shackled to the rock, she thinks of the gods, whom she formerly had praised, as "False and devouring"; the world she had blessed and delighted in as "dark and despiteful." She has no recourse to a higher conception of the world to rationalize her suffering. Kingsley thought of Andromeda as a racial allegory, setting the dark "Aethiop" race against the light, and a gender allegory, setting a woman against a man. Kingsley explained to Ludlow that his focus on Andromeda would emphasize the difference between a Victorian higher consciousness of truth and the pagan myth "without hurting the classicality, by contrasting her tone about the gods with that of Perseus, whom she is ready to worship as being of a higher race; with his golden hair and blue eyes" (*LM,* 2:82).

Because he is interested primarily in Andromeda's education by Perseus and Athene, the poet does not devote much space to the monster, presenting it as a force to be quickly vanquished. A beast with claws, it resembles a great ocean liner: "Onward it came from the southward, as bulky and black as a galley." In six lines, with neither struggle nor suspense, Perseus dispatches the beast:

> Then rushes up with a scream, and stooping the wrath of his eyebrows
> Falls from the sky, like a star, while the wind rattles hoarse in his pinions.

Over him closes the foam for a moment; and then from the sand bed
Rolls up the great fish, dead, and his side gleams white in the sunshine.
Thus fell the boy on the beast, unveiling the face of the Gorgon;
Thus fell the boy on the beast; thus rolled up the beast in his horror,

(16:192)

Andromeda's rescue is not primarily from this beast but from a savage race, marking the moment in history when Greek culture encounters and absorbs the mysterious East.

"Andromeda" is an allegory about the enlightenment of an inferior race. "It happened at Joppa," Kingsley wrote, "and she must have been a Canaanite; and I cannot help fancying that it is some remnant of old human sacrifices to the dark powers of nature, which died out throughout Greece before the higher sunnier faith in *human* gods" (*LM,* 2:82). Dwelling on the Syrian shore, Andromeda comes from barbarians, "dark-haired Aethiop people." "She is a barbarian," explained Kingsley to Ludlow, "and has no notion (beside fetichism) beyond pleasure and pain, as of an animal. It is not till the thinking, sententious Greek, with his awful beauty, inspires her, that she develops into woman" (*LM,* 2:83). Kingsley assimilates the racial story into the gender story, at once educating Andromeda into civilization and true womanhood. At the same time, the dark woman brings to the light man an earthy sexuality. Not blond and blue-eyed but dark and voluptuous, the female Canaanites, Andromeda and her mother Casseopeia, "deep-bosomed wife," boast magnificent heads of raven hair: "down to the ankle her tresses/ Rolled, blue-black as the night, ambrosial, joy to beholders" (174). Sexual attraction thus facilitates gender politics.

Andromeda becomes woman, a civilized, gendered creature, capable of becoming a partner in marriage and bearing noble offspring. The transformation occurs because of love, growing out of "worship and trust, fair parents of love." Perseus needs only to present himself to be adored. A human god, Perseus is lovable for his yellow hair. In its purity and vigor, manliness appears to the maiden as an irresistible dazzling presence:

> Sudden she ceased, with a shriek: in the spray, like a hovering foam-bow,
> Hung, more fair than the foam-bow, a boy in the bloom of his manhood,
> Golden-haired, ivory-limbed, ambrosial; over his shoulder
> Hung for a veil of his beauty the gold-fringed folds of the goat skin, . . .
> Curved on his thigh lay a falchion, and under the gleam of his helmet
> Eyes more blue than the main shone awful; . . .
> Hovering over the water he came, upon glittering pinions,
> Living a wonder
>
> (16:184)

Kingsley defended his emphasis upon the physical wonder of manliness to Ludlow, whose idea of social chivalry did not depend so strongly upon musculature. "Did you ever sit and look at a handsome or well-made man," he asked, "and thank God from your heart for having allowed you such a privilege and lesson?" (*LM,* 2:84). The lesson of male beauty draws Andromeda away from her old and fierce gods.

The barbarian gods practice incest and promote revenge. The dread Queen Atergati of the sea to whom Andromeda is being sacrificed mates with her brother, the Sun. In order to contrast the dark barbaric world with the golden Greek one, Kingsley alters the myth so that the powerful barbarian goddess rather than Poseidon sends the sea monster. He contrasts the incestuous Atergati to Athene, who represents rationality and orderly hierarchies.

The beginning of Andromeda's conversion occurs when she views the erotic play of the water creatures:

> Onward they came in their joy, and around them the lamps of the sea nymphs,
> Myriad fiery globes, swam panting and heaving . . .
> Laughing and singing, and tossing and twining, while eager the Tritons
> Blinded with kisses their eyes, unreproved, and above them in worship

Hovered the terns, and the seagulls swept past them on silvery pinions
Echoing softly their laughter; around them the wantoning dolphins
Sighed as they plunged, full of love; and the great seahorses which bore them
Curved up their crests in their pride to the delicate arms of the maidens,
Pawing the spray into gems, till a fiery rainfall, unharming,
Sparkled and gleamed on the limbs of the nymphs, and the coils of the mermen.

(16:179–80)

The meter here creates what Angus Fletcher defines as symbolic rhythm, which, working against factual statement, "instead creates a kind of incantatory sermon."[46] Enhanced by metrics, the whole ocean scene exalts a moist and gleaming orgy. As in Frost's picture, the nymphs sport around Andromeda who views nature and gods at their wantoning and cries out to the sun god in longing and despair, so that when Perseus arrives the next day she mistakes him for the sun god himself.

As Kingsley meditated for days and weeks about the meaning of the myth, he imagined a maiden exposed to the elements in extreme psychological vulnerability. He pitied her as he wondered how her damp cold condition would limit her eloquence but enhance her receptiveness: "A young girl who has been standing naked in the spray all night, poor little thing, can't spout," he explained. She is thereby made susceptible to a new doctrine: "only when she begins to suspect that this sun god and his vengeance are nothing, she rises to the strength of a new idea" (*LM,* 2:83).

Andromeda, however, does not instantly welcome rescue, the new idea, and the man who embodies them. Cold and wet, she cries for her mother, but Perseus, who views her as valuable in the sexual economy, tames the Aethiop woman to his needs. The entire passage in which Perseus teaches her new worthiness to the trembling maiden is couched in economic metaphors, emphasizing the commodity value of the woman. To the dark barbarians she was only sacrificial food; to Perseus "my prize now." Perseus scorns the "barbarous horde" who devalued her, and wonders at his luck in stumbling on such treasure. His language blends bold adventure with acquisitiveness; chivalric quester has turned into manly capitalist:

> Coward and shameless were he, who so finding a glorious jewel
> Cast on the wayside by fools, would not win it and keep it and wear it,
> Even as I will thee;
>
> (16:186)

By forgiving her mother for willingly sacrificing her daughter to the gods, Andromeda proves that she is malleable and therefore worthy of being won. Perseus first turns the compliant Andromeda against her mother, then he tames her to his desire. Kingsley compares the wooing of Andromeda to the taming of a wild horse:

> Just as at first some colt, wild-eyed, with quivering nostril,
> Plunges in fear of the curb, and the fluttering robes of the rider;
> Soon, grown bold by despair, submits to the will of his master,
> Tamer and tamer each hour, and at last, in the pride of obedience,
> Answers the heel with a curvet, and arches his neck to be fondled,
> Cowed by the need that maid grew tame;
>
> (16:187)

Taming a horse is the properly epic simile for Kingsley who loved a good horse. The conception of wooing here exemplifies Lévi-Strauss' description of woman as an exchange between men, here between two tribes and Gayle Rubin's analysis of marriage as "traffic in women."[47] "Andromeda" exalts that economy as "order and right," sanctified by the wisdom of Aphrodite and Athene. By expressing his views of marriage through the dialogue between Aphrodite and Athene, Kingsley makes the female deities seem complicitous in his patriarchal vision.

Athene is given the role of a stock Kingsley character, the female mentor, a moral guide and support, who appears more expectably in the children's genre of *The Water Babies* (1863), a story about a dirty boy who first becomes clean and then becomes a man through the offices of powerful female teachers.[48] Water babyhood represents a regression in the service of manliness. Tom, an ignorant abused chimney sweep, exists in a state of savagery, having no concept of self to the point of not recognizing himself in a mirror. He turns into a water baby by falling into the water and undergoing a kind of baptism which is a kind of death leading to a rebirth. In their underwater empire Tom progresses from barbarity to manliness through the severe training of the powerful and wise women, Mrs. Doasyouwouldbedoneby and Mrs. Bedonebyasyoudid. Married mentors whose husbands never appear, the matrons alternately love and punish. Tom's final motivation to enter civilization comes from love of Ellie, a golden-haired girl. The story ends with Tom's apotheosis: "he is now a great man of science, and can plan railroads, and steam-engines, and electric telegraphs, and rifled guns and so forth" (19:200). Matrons prepare Tom for technological mastery, his masculine right to dominate the world.

Athene becomes the matronly guide to Perseus and Andromeda, while Andromeda resembles Ellie in *The Water-Babies* and Argemone in *Yeast*. Like Argemone, Andromeda must be educated to her role, and, like Ellie, she is the medium through which Perseus achieves apotheosis as the Victorian paterfamilias. "Andromeda" Eros aids in the conversion of Andromeda to divinely ordained male political aims. Andromeda is sexually aroused first by sporting divinities, then by the spectacle of her beautiful rescuer, and ultimately by her hero's lovemaking. Perseus and Andromeda are caressing, "Answering lip with lip" while Aphrodite blesses their prenuptial rapture as chaste in the context of "espousal." Kingsley praised physical expressions of matrimony to counter the effeminacy of celibate priests. Sex in marriage properly expends manly energy and, more important, shadows divine love.

Speaking for unlicensed eroticism, Aphrodite taunts Athene that her gifts are superior to those of the goddess of wisdom. But Athene counters that she too is a proponent of sexuality; she represents a different form of love, equally committed to heterosexual love, but only in the service of the state:

> Dear unto me, no less than to thee, is the wedlock of heroes;
> Dear, who can worthily win him a wife not unworthy; and noble,
> Pure with the pure to beget brave children, the like of their father.
> Happy, who thus stands linked to the heroes who were, and who shall be;
> Girdled with holiest awe, not sparing of self; for his mother
> Watches his steps with the eyes of the gods; and his wife and his children
> Move him to plan and to do in the farm and the camp and the council.
> Thence comes weal to a nation: but woe upon woe, when the people
> Mingle in love at their will, like the brutes, not heeding the future.
>
> (16:193)

Overseen by his mother, the hero is blessed by marriage, man's highest state on earth and in heaven. Athene's claim echoes the connubial virtues that Kingsley himself exalted. Instituted before the Fall, marriage progresses in Victorian England to its purest form: "towards strict monogamy to more divine, more Scriptural views of marriage than the world has yet seen" (*LM,* 1:197). Fulfilling the promise of Scripture, marriage brings Man as close to God as he can arrive: "The highest state I define as that state through and in which men can know most of God, and work most for God: and this I assert to be the married state" (*LM,* 1:199).

Kingsley invests the married state with increased wisdom, not only enjoyed by the husband but also by the wife. His homage to matronly power extends not only to his fictional characters and to middle-class wives performing social services, but also to wives who write. He develops a concept of feminine criticism as opposed to masculine creativity in a review of Anna Jameson's *Sacred and Legendary Art* (1849).[49] The review praises Jameson for her English Protestant spirit, her effort to preserve the value of Romish art, and her resistance to the seduction of superstitious doctrine. Her femininity enables her to discern truth embedded in the myths and legends distorted or hidden by credulous faith, thereby stripping legends and myths of false trappings, reclaiming their original significance.

Jameson can rescue sacred art from popery not only because she is English and Protestant but because she is a married woman:

> Indeed, for that branch of the subject which she has taken in hand, not the history, but the poetry of legends and of the art which they awakened, she derives a peculiar fitness, not merely from her own literary talents and acquaintance with continental art, but also from the very fact of her being an English wife and mother.[50]

Like Mrs. Bedonebyasyoudid and Mrs. Doasyouwouldbedoneby, Mrs. Jameson is a matronly mentor. As the manchild matures she leads him to appreciation, what Kingsley calls criticism:

> Women ought, perhaps, always to make the best critics—at once more quicksighted, more tasteful, more sympathetic than ourselves, whose proper business is creation . . . But of all critics an English matron ought to be the best—open as she should be, by her womanhood, to all tendner and admiring sympathies, accustomed by her Protestant education to unsullied purity of thought, and inheriting from her race, not only freedom of mind and reverence for antiquity, but the far higher birthright of English honesty.[51]

Not an empty title, "Mrs." signifies Anna Jameson's qualifications. Marriage nurtures sympathy, allowing the matron to extract purity from dross, truth from exaggeration. Tender sympathy teaches married women to interpret, and thereby to preserve the culture man creates. Kingsley's "Introductory Lecture" at Queen's College (1848), in which he defended woman's education, defines the advantages of matronly interpretation:

> always to find her highest interest in mankind, simply as mankind, to see the Divine most completely in the human; to prefer the incarnate to the disembodied, the personal to the abstract . . . to see in the most common tale of village love or

> sorrow, a mystery deeper and more divine than lies in all the theories of politician or the fixed ideas of the sage.[52]

Woman accept immanence, finding in what is tangible and palpable its unbodied essence. With her ability to interpret facts, the matrons find divine meaning in the material world.

In "Andromeda" Kingsley made Athene into the wise woman who finds meaning in the incarnate. By giving Hephaestos' epic role in forging heroic arms to Athene who weaves the wedding veil, Kingsley transforms war epic to marriage epic. To create the character of Athene, Kingsley conflated two women's roles in classical epic, that of the maternal Thetis, who conveys arms to her son Achilles, and that of the woman as weaver, exemplified by both Helen and Penelope. As goddess of the loom, Athene weaves the wedding veil, fashioning it as Hephaestos forged Achilles' shield in *The Iliad.* In "Andromeda" Hephaestos crafts wedding jewels for the bride, not mighty weapons for the warrior; Athene's wedding veil for Andromeda imitates Hepaestos' wondrous shield for Achilles encompassing all of Creation in its images:

> In it she wove all creatures that teem in the womb of the ocean,
> Nereid, siren, and triton, and dolphin, and arrowy fishes . . .
> In it she wove, too, a town where grey-haired kings sat in judgment;
> Sceptre in hand in the market they sat, doing right by the people,
> Wise: while above watched Justice, and near, far-seeing Apollo.
> Round it she wove for a fringe all herbs of the earth and the water,
> Violet, asphodel, ivy, and vine-leaves, roses and lilies,
> Coral and sea-fan and tangle, the blooms and the palms of the ocean:
>
> (16:195)

The transfer of this ekphrastic passage from a poem of war to a poem of marriage represents the feminization of epic, the Victorian domestication of heroic values. His wife's wedding veil is the manly Christian's shield.

Rescue raises Andromeda to marriage and a view of her place in the economic hierarchy. Athene teaches her pupil a more exalted view of her role, and Kingsley presents the wife as enabling the husband a vision of the Lord. Through family ties, Kingsley argues, "God reveals Himself to man, and reveals man's relations to Him." Kingsley argues by analogy: "Fully to understand the meaning of 'a Father in Heaven' we must be fathers ourselves; to know how Christ loved the Church, we must have wives to love, and love them" (*LM,* 1:199). Andromeda's reward for governing herself, her house, and her people and bearing a "god-like race to thy spouse" is to shine all night as "a star in the heavens" and to feast all day with the Olympian gods, seated next to her husband, the "god-begotten" (16:196).

Like Athena in the *Oresteia,* Athene in "Andromeda" conveys patriarchal values, asserting the proper gender hierarchy, and in her wisdom, sharing Aphrodite's province of Eros and Ares' province of War:

> Chanting of valour and fame, and the man who can fall with the foremost
> Fighting for children and wife, and the field which his father bequeathed him."
>
> (16:197)

Athene sings of gender hierarchy, marriage, war, and the male ownership of property. The goddess is wise because she not only expresses but reproduces and enforces the conventional order.

Kingsley's manliness appropriates maternal interpretation to serve male authority. Unmindful of its contradictions, he reiterates his message, revealing some discomfort at his own assertions in his frequent undermining of them. Lancelot Smith is haunted by a sense of his own unworthiness: "daily his self-confidence and sense of rightful power developed, and with them, paradoxical as it may seem, the bitterest self-abasement" (15:124). Kingsley's valuation of manliness is similarly contradictory. Manliness at once purifies and pollutes. "Andromeda" presents its happy ending as resolving the conflict in marriage. In his meditations on the meaning of the Saint George legend, however, Kingsley adds to the marriage allegory of the Greek myth an allegory of pollution.

In puzzling over the historical basis for the St. George legend, Kingsley seemingly dismissed an allegorical interpretation that was nonetheless close to his own social concerns. St. George slaying the dragon and Apollo battling Python were not a fabulist's hallucinations but tales of manly socialism in action. "Why should not these dragons have been simply what the Greek word dragon means," he asked, "'mighty worms' huge snakes?" After a long meditation on the existence of huge snakes in remains of dinosaurs, the "Pterodactylus," to its becoming a manifestation of evil to Christian and ancient Hebrew, Kingsley seems to scoff at a euhemeristic interpretation: "the theory that the tales of Hercules and the Hydra, Apollo and the mud-Python, St. George and the Dragon, were sanitary reform allegories, and the monsters whose poisonous breath destroyed cattle and young maidens only typhus and consumption."[53]Kingsley's concern with disease and dirt is congruent with his antipollution crusade. As a man who became distraught from a spot on his trousers, he hoped his working men would learn to bathe daily.[54] Kingsley favors the theory that the snake-gods were met by Christian heroes, imagining himself as one of those heroes, fighting filth in eloquent tracts about sanitary reform. "Every one of you," he exhorted the Ladies Sanitary Association, "can find" . . . a chivalrous work to do—just as chivalrous as if you lived in any old magic land, such as Spenser talked of in his Faery Queene . . . "[55] In their way women can emulate St. George. To the Ladies Sanitary Association Spenser's hero is the model for fighting against typhus and consumption.

The two versions of the myth enabled Kingsley to present his social program as eternal truth, figured allegorically. Together the two stories purify sexual and excremental filth. Both wise woman and wife in "Andromeda" avoid the deaths reserved for other Kingsley heroines. Argemone dies of typhus, although her last name—Lavington—indicates the importance of washing. Hypatia, the rational virgin philosopher and teacher, has her naked body rent limb by limb, as her wails "thrilled like the trumpet of avenging angels." Her martyrdom occurs "right underneath the great still Christ" (10:212). "Saint Maura," written the same year as "Andromeda," features a pregnant woman who is martyred by public stripping and flagellation.

Although the final scene of "Andromeda" seeks closure, its ending contradicts the meaning of marriage as purification. Alone in her chamber while the other gods and goddesses rejoice at the nuptials, Athene weaves pictures of nature appropriated for patriarchal values. Unlike the rescued maiden, however, Athene's virginity is not destined to be given up for male ownership and procreation: "Happy, who hearing her obey her the wise unsullied Athene" (16:197). Like the other women mentors, Athene plans new lessons for mortals, recommending marriage. But she is not a Mrs.; she is "unsullied." On the one hand, Kingsley despises celibacy and sanctifies carnality; on the other, he associates carnality with being sullied. His characteristic association of cleanliness with female chastity reinscribes the virginity he derided in Catholic worship of the Virgin Mary.[56] Athene substitutes for that virgin, but she is the daughter not the son of a male god. Interpreting the moral world to mortals sullied by sexuality, the virgin goddess who denied having a mother mothers Kingsley's manliness.

Hopkins' Female Monster

HOPKINS' SONNET "Andromeda," written in 1879, is his only poem on a Greek myth. Drawing upon a tradition that began in the Middle Ages, Hopkins allegorizes the story to adapt pagan myth to Christian belief. He may have been aware of Boccaccio's *Genealogy of the Gods* where Perseus is allegorically interpreted as a symbol of Christ, but he could just as well have been influenced by other authors who interpreted Perseus as allegorical of Christ.[57] In Hopkins' allegory Perseus is Christ, Andromeda is the Church, and the Dragon is contemporary wickedness. This deployment of figures is in the same tradition as Alexander Ross' *Mystagogus Poeticus, or The Muses Interpreter:*

> Our blessed Saviour is the true Perseus, the Son of the true God, and of a pure Virgin, exposed in his infancy, and all his life after to many dangers; he hath subdued all our spiritual *Gor-*

> *gons,* and hath delivered the Church his fair Spouse, from the Devil, that great monster, who was ready to devour her; at last having conquered all his enemies, he hath ascended into glory, and there hath prepared a place for his *Andromeda,* the Church.[58]

Unlike Ross, however, Hopkins emphasizes the temporal relevance of the myth's Christian meaning: "Now, Time's Andromeda" (50, l. 1). As the temporal Church founded on this Rock, Andromeda suffers a long history of persecution. Once more she is being assaulted. Hopkins focuses not on the dragon slaying but upon the moment before Perseus descends. He suspends the action as Perseus, like the windhover, hangs in the air, observing the drama below him. This is the maiden's grimmest hour; the dragon advances. She does not know that her rescue is imminent. At the moment in history of the poem, the specific dragon, unlike Ross', has not been slain. However, the narrative certainty that Perseus will descend, slay the dragon, and deliver the maiden imbues the Christian allegory with the inevitability of the Greek myth. The myth's story of rescue confirms religious faith. Salvation will come; the evil will be vanquished, not in the afterlife, but here, in the world.

The first line establishes that Hopkins is making both a doctrinal allegory, as in Ross' mythography, and a topical allegory. The Church, "With not her either beauty's equal or/Her injury's" (ll. 2–3), once again, is being attacked in Victorian England by some unnamed horror which promises if unchecked to consume the Church. Hopkins dwells on the scene of attack: the maiden chained to the rude rock of Peter's Church because of her loveliness appears helpless in face of the current onslaught: "Her flower, her piece of being, doomed dragon food" (l. 4).

The poet makes concrete the dragon's threat of incorporating the Church, imagining the maiden as a toothsome morsel for the monster, the imagery comprehending sexuality (in the conventional female emblem of the flower), fragmentation (in referring to the maiden's entire being as a piece), and incorporation. By calling Andromeda's entire being a piece, Hopkins suggests that a specific portion, vital to the Church's survival, is being threatened.[59] The dragon incorporates the maiden by eating her, becoming a distorting mirror of her, perverting what it has eaten. The monster, as a form of Satan, in trying to eat the maiden parodies, and therefore blasphemes, the Mass.[60]

Hopkins emphasizes the unruly hunger of this monster; it is wild, suggestive of primitive need, existing beneath culture. In addition, the assonance of "doom" and "food" give to taking nourishment a ghastly judgmental quality. The dragon is unmistakably terrible, its threat apparently never more virulent than in these times. In a snap and virtually in the next second, the demonic creature will incorporate the church. Hopkins imagines the monster as impelled not only by the sin of greed but also by lust.

This maiden Church's "piece" is enduring the ultimate trial, the greatest threat to date. Considering the indignities the Church has suffered from Roman times, through Reformation, to the Enlightenment, Hopkins makes an extremely strong statement:

> Time past she has been attempted and pursued
> By many blows and bones; but now hears roar
> A wilder beast from West than all were, more
> Rife in her wrongs, more lawless, and more lewd.
> (ll. 5–8)

The few critics who have commented on the poem have only broadly speculated about what the wilder beast represents. The Gardner and Mackenzie notes to the poems, for example, express their uncertainty by retreating to the passive voice: "The symbolism of this sonnet, clearly suggested in the first line, is tentatively elucidated . . . " and explicate the seventh line thus "the new powers of Antichrist, which for G. M. H. would include rationalism, Darwinism, industrialism, the new paganism of Swinburne and Whitman, possibly Nietzsche" (*Poems,* p. 277). The ills of these abstract "isms," culled from many things Hopkins had railed against and from some standard Victorian insecurities, touch upon many problems, but Hopkins is usually quite specific about what distresses him, for example, in "God's Grandeur" or "Binsey Poplars."

In fact, the Church was once again under serious assault. The Higher Criticism caused many to loose their faith, while it brought others, Hopkins among them, to the Catholic Church. Hopkins followed with interest Bishop Colenso's trial for the heresy of examining the Pentateuch historically.[61] He himself believed that he entered the Roman Church on the basis of its claims to authority.[62]

More relevant to the time of Hopkins' composing "Andromeda" is the "new paganism." Pater was one of his teachers and was associated with a new turn, bordering on devotion, to paganism. Hopkins continued to visit Pater after his conversion in 1866. "Pater was one of the men I saw most of," Hopkins remarked in 1879, the year in which he wrote "Andromeda." At that time Pater was thinking about particular mythological subjects and Greek civilization in general. In 1875 he delivered two lectures on "The Myth of Demeter and Persephone," publishing them in the *Fortnightly Review* the following year; that same year he published "The Study of Dionysus." At the same time he probably wrote "The Bacchanals of Euripides," not published until 1889. The year before Hopkins wrote "Andromeda," in 1878, Pater revised the four essays, possibly intending to publish them as a volume.[63] Pater proposed that Greek myths express a universal pagan sentiment and that Greek deities could be useful in modern times. As an antidote to a "mechanical conception" of the natural world held by "modern science," Pater places the more "unmechanical, spiritual, or Platonic" philosophy. A sense of a "personal intelligence" that abides in the world might be derived from reconsideration of, even belief in, the meaning of classical myth.[64]

Allegorical depictions, Pater suggests, when animated by understanding, derive from a "Greek" sensibility:

> symbolical representations, under the form of human persons, as Giotto's *Virtues* and *Vices* at Padua, or his *Saint Poverty* at Assisi . . . seem to be something more than mere symbolism, and to be connected with some peculiarly sympathetic penetration, on the part of the artist, into the subjects he intended to depict.[65]

Pater does not think that Greek myth arose from historical fact but from pure ideas. Rather than reporting historical events (what Kingsley believed), Greek myth contains "adequate symbols" of mankind's "deepest thoughts concerning the conditions of his physical and spiritual life."[66] Greek myth can be used by contemporary art to bring into culture what is being lost by a mechanical view of nature. Animated by deep sympathy with the breathing world beyond the self, allegory could bring to Victorians a deepened belief and awe.

The new paganism in its extreme forms might threaten the Church, but Hopkins gives no indication that he thought Pater's ideas so destructive as to warrant the language of his sonnet.[67] On the contrary, Hopkins may have been inspired by Pater's opinions in 1868–69 to write his only poem on a Greek myth. Pater's appreciation for myth's symbolic potential could sugget to Hopkins a way of reinterpreting Andromeda, not according to Pater's aestheticism but according to those religious symbols that were profoundly meaningful to his own religious views.

Why this poem in 1879? Rationalism was not new; industrialism was spreading, and Hopkins wrote about the earth being despoiled by pollution. The black West of "God's Grandeur" corresponds on one level to the wilder Western beast in "Andromeda." Specific words in the poem and Hopkins' attitudes at the time of the poem's composition point to specific concerns, suggested by his notes to Bridges about the sonnet and also by his letters to friends about current events.

Hopkins sent his "Andromeda" to Bridges, inviting criticism and telling him that he aimed at a "more Miltonic plainness and severity than I have anywhere else." His allusion to Milton may refer to more than style. The inversions and coinages, particularly in the last line, seem more Hopkinsian than Miltonic. In fact, the poem is only marginally more spare in its style, a fact that Hopkins acknowledged: "I cannot say that it has turned out severe, still less plain, but it seems almost free from quaintness and in aiming at one excellence I may have hit another."[68] The other excellence is not only in the style but in the conception of the evils besetting the church. Hopkins may have taken inspiration from Milton to use the sonnet form to comment on the meeting of morality, politics, and the social condition. "Miltonic plainness," then, refers to being plainspoken, political, and topical.

Hopkins' allusion to Milton is also relevant to the sonnet's figuration of the monster. The Victorian sonnet's presentation of evil alludes thematically and figurally to Milton's epic poem, to the fallen world and to the cause of its falling. Hopkins allies himself with his English heritage through Milton back to Spenser. His dragon with its lewd ungovernable appetite and unparalleled threat resembles the complex origins of Milton's Sin in *Paradise Lost.*[69] Spenser's Errour in *The Fairie Queene,* one of Milton's sources for Sin, is a foul mother whose offspring "Of sundrie shapes, yet all ill favored" retreat into the monster's mouth (*FQ* I. i. xv). Like Hopkins' monster Errour conflates eating with sexual appetite. The Red-Cross Knight, who is a version of St. George,[70] encounters the part-serpent in a half-gloom, hacking off the beast's head, as Perseus had done to Medusa's, conflating the classical hero's two battles with monsters.

Like Milton's and Spenser's serpent-woman, Hopkins' beast is not only female but lewd.[71] Hopkins alludes to her sex and her sexuality in a few short, generally overlooked, words: "more/ Rife in her wrongs, more lawless, and more lewd." The allegorical tradition upon which Hopkins was drawing gave him ample precedent for the female serpent.[72] In Satan's confrontation with Sin Milton presents a perverted relationship between parent and child, Father and Daughter/Mother incestuously using each other.[73] The extremity of Hopkins' claim for his beast takes some of its authority from the depth of Milton's and Spenser's conception of her. Error and Sin pervert and yet mirror the ideal promise of divinity. By using the St. George/Perseus myth implicit in *The Fairie Queene,* Hopkins imports into "Andromeda" the horror of his precursors' imaginings. Hopkins' female beast owes its conception to representations of Satan as a serpent with a female head and to the tradition which imagined that monster as female.[74] Indeed, so multilayered is the tradition that has given a female gender to sin and has connected that gender with vile, odorous sexuality and generation that Hopkins could simply be imitating "Miltonic plainness" in so representing his wild beast.

In addition to figuring his poem in such a way as to emulate his literary predecessors, Hopkins alludes to events of his day, employing the myth to represent the gender conflicts of his times, figuring those conflicts in a traditional religious allegory. Much was occurring in the years up to and preceding 1879 that might have impelled Hopkins into this particular allegorical figuration of this particular myth. Commentators have mentioned many reasons for Hopkins to believe that the church was being ultimately threatened, but none that would call for a specifically female monster, although the times experienced an unprecedented drive for female emancipation. The scaly wings of the female beast, displaying her sexuality and attacking the sanctity of the virgin church with her lewd, ungoverned desires challenged the bright wings of the male Holy Ghost who brooded over the bent world.

The controversy about laws governing women and sexual behavior invaded traditionally male precincts—Church, Law, Medicine—as angels in their sanctified houses doffed their wings to walk the streets. They insisted upon the rights of the (male) body politic—of their right within patriarchy to own property independent of their husbands—and upon the rights of their bodies—of their right within patriarchy to use birth control, to refuse genital examination if they were suspected of carrying venereal disease. They wanted the vote. Abigail Bloomer insisted upon her right to wear pants.

Hopkins presented his Miltonic sonnet to Bridges at the end of a decade in which social changes challenged traditional relations between the sexes. Fraser Harrison observes that "women and men alike were obliged to come to terms with changes in almost all aspects of their social and economic life; none was more disturbing and carried further-reaching implications than the radical alteration in relationships between the sexes."[75] As a priest Hopkins was acutely pained by the way legal changes hampered the church's authority to regulate the gender hierarchy. Women gained increasing independence from male authority, particularly within marriage. To survey, however briefly, the occurrences "now," in 1878–79, is to notice social and legal acts that radically changed the relation between the sexes at the time Hopkins wrote his sonnet.

In the ten years before 1879 the agitation for women's suffrage and her ownership of property was beginning to give women some independence from their husbands. In 1870, after twenty years of effort, the first Married Women's Property Act passed, allowing wives to retain personal earnings from employment. At the end of the decade, after ten years of agitation, the Royal Commission considered repeal or amendment of the Contagious Diseases Act, an act allowing the examination and detention of women suspected of carrying venereal disease.

Josephine Butler was particularly active during this time on behalf of the prostitutes and poor working women of Liverpool and remarked at a hearing that the men who supported the prostitutes' trade were at least as culpable as the impoverished women who practiced it. In 1878 the Matrimonial Causes Act allowed a woman to separate from her husband for assault. In the same year Annie Besant and Charles Bradlaugh won a legal victory to stop authorities' century-old policy of proscribing birth-control literature. Bradlaugh and Besant sold "Fruits of Philosophy," a pamphlet by the American physician Dr. Charles Knowlton arguing in favor of birth control and clearly explaining the use of various contraceptive devices.

Hopkins was aware of the changing climate which permitted the sale of the pamphlet and which was also reflected in the 1857 law removing divorce from the jurisdiction of the ecclesiastical courts to a new secular Divorce Court. Commenting on current events in the same year he wrote "Andromeda," he expressed his horror to his friend Alexander William Mowbray Baillie in language that links campaigning for birth control with the work of the devil:

> Bradlaugh spoke here lately and Mrs. Annie Besant gave 3 lectures on Sunday last. To think I could ever have called myself a Liberal! "The Devil was the first Whig." These two are at large (I mean Bradlaugh and Besant) and the Government is arresting Irish agitators, that will do far more harm in prison than on the stump.[76]

Hopkins wrote the letter from Manchester, with sympathy for the sufferings of his faithful but with horror at the forces which threatened authority. As in "Andromeda," the forces of evil are wildly overrunning the land, they are "at large," out of control, but with legal sanction. By refusing to jail Bessant and Bradlaugh the Government seems in collusion with the Devil.

In 1879 Frances Mary Buss founded the first public day school for girls, and London University offered all its degrees and prizes to women. With some ability to keep their income and wages, educated wives could disturb the hierarchy sacred to marriage by defying their husband's injunctions. Women independent from men were worse. Hopkins envisioned them as enemies of religion, as temptresses. In 1879, as part of an ongoing campaign to reclaim Bridges, if not for the Catholic Church, at least for Christianity or, failing that, at least as believer in the true God, he recounted an anecdote which polarizes sexual temptations of women against the beauty of Church doctrine:

> For here something applies like the French Bishop's question to his clergy whenever one of them came to have intellectual difficulties and must withdraw from the exercise of his priestly functions—*What is her name?*[77]

In Hopkins' sonnet the purity of women and the power of man, both sacred to ecclesiastical authority, is menaced by an impure "lewd" female. Employing the conventional opposition between virgin and whore, Hopkins transforms the lewd female into a monster. He associates the beast with hordes of rebellious peasants, much as Milton and Spenser had done when they allegorized the progeny of Sin and Error.

Hopkins attitudes toward marriage, particularly the authority of Church and husband over the wife, are more explicit in his correspondence with the poet Coventry Patmore, a convert to Catholicism two years before Hopkins. In the 1880s Patmore was revising his *The Angel in the House* which he had published before his conversion. Hopkins assiduously read the work and suggested emendations, partly metrical but doctrinal as well. Hopkins asked that Patmore reconsider his slackness in regard to the gender hierarchy in marriage. At one point in *The Angel in the House,* Patmore comments, apparently approvingly, that the wife calls her husband "lord" "by courtesy":

> Because, although in act and word
>   As lowly as a wife can be,
> Her manners when they call me lord,
>   Remind me 'tis by courtesy;

Not with her least consent of will,
  Which would my proud affection hurt,
But by the noble style that still
  Imputes an unattain'd desert.[78]

Hopkins addresses himself to the difference between conviction and courtesy as the sort of severe lapse that will inevitably lead to grave consequences, undermining the foundation of the Church:

> Naturally a lurking error appears in more places than one and a false principle gives rise to false consequences. An ideal becomes an idol and false worship sets in. So I call it . . . where it is said that a wife calls her husband lord by courtesy, meaning, as I understand, only by courtesy and "not with her least consent of will" to his being so. But he *is* her lord. If it is by courtesy only and no consent then a wife's lowliness is hypocrisy and Christian marriage a comedy, a piece of pretence.[79]

Based upon hierarchy, Christian marriage depends on woman's subservience to her lord as man is subservient to his Lord. Correspondence between wife and sinner, lord and Lord, is a system facilitating allegorical representation. Wives' politeness compares to religiosity rather than to true belief. Since domestic hierarchy is analogous to the Church's temporal authority, a wife's mere courtesy compares to the undermining of the Church:

> And now pernicious doctrines and practice are abroad and the other day the papers said a wretched being refused in church to say the words "and obey." If it had been a Catholic wedding and I the priest I would have let the sacrilege go no further.[80]

Hopkins can call the wretched being neither woman nor bride. "Andromeda" cries out with similar outrage, positioning the "wretched being" and "wilder beast" as parallel terms.

The pernicious doctrine ravaging the countryside is personified in a lewd beast who will not vow to be subservient. Patmore took this lecture to heart, for in 1887 he wrote in repentance two articles for the *St. James's Gazette* in which he attacked the new doctrines about the equality of women in words that echo Hopkins' sonnet. Entitled "The Weaker Vessel" and "Why Women are Dissatisfied," he first invokes Milton's prescription of woman's obedience to her lord: "He for God only, She for God in him." Patmore begins his article with the force of a commandment. He is about to define a dogma and to speak against a heresy: "Now," he says, using the same word that began Hopkins' sonnet, "it is high time that it should be plainly declared that there are few more damnable heresies than the doctrine of the equality of man and woman. It strikes at the root of the material and spiritual prosperity and felicity of both, and vitiates the whole life of society in its source."[81] Patmore's language echoes the sentiments of "Andromeda": "Time past she has been attempted and pursued": "From time to time in the world's past history, the inferiority and consequent subordination of woman have been denied by some fanatic or insignificant sect of fanatics, and the cudgels have been taken up for man by some busybody in his premature dread of the monstrous regiment of women; but the consensus of the world has until lately been dead against the notion."[82] Until now, claims Patmore, the agitation of women for equality could be silenced; it was a fit of hysterics to be calmed by manly reason. Like Hopkins, Patmore conceives of the women's movement as monstrous. Patmore's articles call for male heroism to rescue confused women from their "dissatisfaction," a word implying petulance rather than grievance. Women are dissatisfied because men have abdicated their strong role and abandoned women without moorings and without their natural ruler, their lords. Undermining firm gender categories weakens the whole of society.

Hopkins' Andromeda myth counteracts feminist agitation of his time; by 1879 the myth had become a Victorian cipher for gender politics, useful for reinscribing traditional authority. Its figures represent the proper hierarchy of man and woman; in Hopkins' allegory, as in Patmore's diatribe, the relation between ruling man and subservient woman is analogous to the relation between the Lord and his creatures.

Hopkins places Christ in the role of chivalric gentleman—as he had done before ("oh my chevalier," "The Windhover")—and represents divinity as ideal manliness. Perseus seems a pensive, even reticent hero, who acts only at the last minute:

> Her Perseus linger and leave her to her extremes?—
> Pillowing air he treads a time and hangs
> His thoughts on her, forsaken that she seems.
>
> (ll. 9–11)

The answer to the question is not obvious; Perseus does indeed seem to linger. Since the English Church had not yet been saved, allegorical imperatives might seem to require such drawing out of the maiden's torture, but others such as Etty had imagined Perseus as racing to Andromeda's rescue rather than treading the air in contemplation of the worst assault the Church had ever known. While Perseus lingers, Andromeda learns the martyr's lesson of patience through torment: "All the while her patience morselled into pangs/ Mounts . . ." (l. 12).

Ending his poem with a vision of the future when the true Perseus will deliver England from false ecclesiastical authority, Hopkins includes a reference to the Medusa: "With Gorgons gear" the hero alights. But Perseus possesses more than Gorgon's head as weapon. As he disables Andromeda's enemy, the ambiguity of the word "disarming" suggests also the glory of the rescuer:

> Then to alight disarming, no one dreams
> With Gorgon's gear and barebill/ thongs and fangs.
>
> (ll. 13–14)

Hopkins imagines Perseus, at once chivalric St. George and Christ, as a charming savior. The poet uses the slain temptress against the lewd monster, with the courtesy of the manly hero controlling the wildness of two bestial females. In Hopkins' name, which he perhaps unconsciously echoes in his praise of self-control and the masculine ideal,[83] "manly" is an essential term preserving the distinction between female maiden and monster.

CHAPTER THREE
Typologies of Defloration

N 1849 Dante Gabriel Rossetti's eyes and ears recorded what the nostalgia of young men might consider romantic. With an antiquarian's energy, he combed old books in the British Museum collections to unearth signs of earlier days. "I have done but little in any way," he told his brother William Michael, then immediately belied his languishing pose, "having wasted several days at the Museum where I have been reading up all manner of old romaunts, to pitch upon stunning words for poetry. I have found several."[1] Rossetti presents himself as an armchair knight questing to capture words for picturesque yet arresting poetry.

Rossetti wants his poetry to "stun"—a favored Pre-Raphaelite word, referring to women as well as to words. The words he seeks with offhand assiduousness contribute to a poetics that masks preoccupation about female sexuality with antique decoration. In his double sonnets "For Ruggiero and Angelica by Ingres" (1848), he uses some antique words to evoke a foreign renaissance past as a way of recreating Ariosto's rescue scene, adapted from Ovid. Rossetti filters through the lens of Ariosto's romance and Ingres' romantic painting the intense fleshly experience he saw symbolized in the rescue scene. The old romance that Rossetti created out of the Andromeda myth, made fascinating with stunning words, expresses concern, even anxiety, about sexual initiation. Yet his ekphrastic sonnets seem simply to describe someone else's painting about someone else's poem, simply retelling a story, adding nothing new, as William Morris similarly presents his poet, "an idle singer of an empty day."

Rossetti galvanized his followers, first those who formed the Pre-Raphaelite Brotherhood, and then the younger William Morris and Edward Burne-Jones. To distinguish the later group from the earlier Pre-Raphaelites, I call them "Aesthetics," a term used in admiration by Walter Pater, Algernon Charles Swinburne, and Oscar Wilde. Robert Buchanan used the same term, but derogatively, in an infamous review where the critic deplores how the "Fleshly School" used typology to obscure the distinction between good and bad women.[2] In fact, both Buchanan and Pater recognized that under Rossetti's influence the Aesthetics used a typological method. By creating a typological progression which aligned stories of women at a turning point in their sexual lives, the Aesthetics explored sexual boundaries, the boundary between sexual innocence and experience but also the boundary distinguishing one gender from another.

Contemporary critics such as Buchanan and Pater recognized that Aesthetic revisionist typology collapsed into a common ground what ordinarily had been kept separate. Buchanan's judgment against the Fleshly School attempts to police the borderline between good and bad women. The critic's very rigidity suggests he was partly aware of the precarious distinctions he was defending. Challenging conventional pieties, the Aesthetics frequently ignore traditional distinctions. Clear outlines and scrupulous fidelity to details in Pre-Raphaelite paintings belie the Aesthetic undermining of the idea of outline itself. The Aesthetics probe boundaries by focusing on intense emotional moments when what seem firm categories become fluid. The line between innocent and experienced women, a way of making moral judgments, becomes an area of confusing similarities.

Because typological ordering draws parallels between apparently unlike stories and unlike systems of belief, it provided the Aesthetics with a congenial interpretative strategy, making possible the blurring of distinctions. Its origin in a traditionally religious hermeneutic casts a sacred aura upon the Aesthetics' work, disguising their revisionary use of typological symbolism. Reversing the Church Fathers' project of interpreting the physical world to accord with a spiritual meaning, Aesthetic typology erases distinctions between body and soul.

Aesthetic poems and paintings of the Andromeda myth modify and extend biblical typological models to draw a parallel between Andromeda's rescue scene and the annunciation scene in Mary's bedroom or garden, imparting a contemporary meaning to both pagan and religious stories. The Aesthetics represent the slaying and rescuing in the Andromeda myth as symbolic of the maiden's defloration. That moment, troubling as well as fascinating to the Aesthetics, is a threshold event which first blurs and then clarifies sexual difference.

Although they portray the act of love as an act of violence, Aesthetic representations appear playful; the supernatural creatures seem decorative, almost entirely drained of danger. This disjunction between interpretation and representation has frequently been misunderstood as a lack of rigorous training or thinking.[3] Such criticism ignores the effects of Aesthetic disjunctions, blurred distinctions, and strange perspectives. In their many representations of Perseus/St. George what seems to be careless, decorative adaptation of typology permits the Aesthetics to explore new territories, to question a sexual topic that had previously been considered sacrosanct, and to disguise their concerns about their own questioning. They disturb a culturally accepted connection between purity and virginity, implicitly challenging the distinction between flesh and spirit.[4] The Aesthetics' typological representations, as this chapter will argue, turn the Andromeda myth into a story of crossing, even transgressing, a cultural boundary.

Chaste and Unchaste Women

BUCHANAN USED the scornful epithet "fleshly" in his 1871 review, "The Fleshly School of Poetry: Mr. D. G. Rossetti," to deplore the Aesthetic transformation of spirituality into carnality. To Buchanan Rossetti's practice of merging physical with spiritual characteristics seemed impious if not heretical, particularly when referring to women. To categorize women without preserving a dualistic moral scale was reason enough for Buchanan to discredit the poet: "Whether he is writing of the holy Damozel, or of the Virgin herself, or of Lilith, or Helen . . . he is fleshly all over, never spiritual, never tender; always self-conscious and aesthetic."[5] Buchanan's prudery disguises his affinity to those he attacks. He reacts against Rossetti and his school not simply because their poetry repels him but partly because it fascinates him. Rosetti overheats Buchanan's imagination; the poet's "offensive mode" in which lovers, "bite, scratch, scream, bubble, munch, sweat, writhe, twist, wriggle, foam, and slaver" apparently forces the critic to imagine the blessed damozel or perhaps the Virgin herself engaging in such activities. The offended critic then pines for pre-evolutionary times:

> One cannot help wishing that things had remained for ever in the asexual state described in Mr. Darwin's great chapter on Palingenesis. We get very weary of this protracted hankering after a person of the other sex; it seems meat, drink, thought, sinew, religion for the fleshly school. There is no limit to the fleshliness, and Mr. Rossetti finds in it its own religious justification.[6]

Buchanan's aesthetic tone, particularly evident in his use of "weary" to describe himself, betrays some identification with those whom he castigates, as does his evident pleasure in repeating fleshly passages. Buchanan's epithet refers to Rossetti's tendency to sanctify his preoccupation with the mechanics of sexual activity, but the critic failed to appreciate that, in addition to youthful carnality, fleshliness represented emotional states that others preferred to leave inchoate. Aesthetic fleshliness could capture the turmoil of a body under its most fearful yet desirous moments.

At a period in history where sexual difference was strongly reaffirmed, fleshliness enabled Rossetti and his Aesthetic disciples to question the fixities of those differences. Rather than a firm agreement of what is man and what is woman, the Aesthetics make those basic dualities problematic, exposing them as somewhat arbitrary polar extremes which cannot always be forced apart but sometimes merge and become indistinguishable. The figural counterpart of that merging is their characteristically androgynous images, which deny, or at least mute, sexual differences.[7] Supernatural creatures, such as the monsters in the Andromeda myth, also exhibit androgynous characteristics by performing male and female functions.

Buchanan's assessment, then, is not inaccurate. Fleshliness is an essential component of Mr. Rossetti's religion, not only in an aesthetic sense but also in his revision of a typological method of interpretation.[8] Rossetti's Virgin Mary engaging in fleshly activities shocked Buchanan, but that concept was a simple, if important, modification of typological interpretations, many of which Rossetti encountered in his readings in the British Museum. In scolding Rossetti for placing all manner of women on the same symbolic plane—the Virgin herself with Lilith or Helen—Buchanan apparently did not recognize the venerable tradition behind such categorization.

Earlier centuries did not always classify women according to degrees of virtue but compared Lilith, Helen, and the Virgin Mary. Thomas Heywoode's *Gynaikion or Nine Books of Various History Concerning Women* (1624), a book in Rossetti's library as well as in the Reading Room of the British Museum,[9] recounted stories according to nine different categories of women; one book for each of the nine Muses. In the sixth book, "Erato—Treating of Chast Women and of Women Wantons," Heywoode explains that the two types of women belong in the same category, are patrons of the same muse: "Erato, signifying Love, both being lovers—one of virtue the other of Vice."[10] Rossetti's ethereal women—

his Beatrices, maidens, and virgins—in Heywoode's schema are one aspect of Erato; Jenny, Lilith, and the femmes fatales of his later paintings are the other. Angelica—his Romantic Andromeda—poises on the threshold between the two, as does his Mary Virgin.

Rossetti's dramatic monologue, "Jenny," meditates upon the meaning of this threshold, the speaker thinking of sexual categories of women in terms of Heywoode's pure and impure women. In considering the concerns of pretty young women, their fondness for fun, variety, and praise, the poem's musing speaker finds more than superficial similarities between Jenny, the young streetwalker, and his undoubtedly respectable cousin Nell. Gazing at the sleeping Jenny's face, he thinks not only of his cousin but also of representations of "pure" women, specifically of Raphael's Virgins:

> Fair shines the gilded aureole
> In which our highest painters place
> Some living woman's simple face.[11]

The sleeping Jenny resembles Raphael's representations of the Virgin. Rossetti notices the disparity between representation and life. Art can represent purity even though the artist may employ an impure model. Raphael's vigins, he suggests, could have been modeled by actual streetwalkers.[12] This perception challenges the distinction between chaste and unchaste women and between chaste and unchaste art. Both Jenny and Nell are fond of money; Raphael's "virgins," like Dante Gabriel's models, sold their faces to the artist; the artist in turn sold his paintings of them as virgins. How then, does one represent the difference, or, more disturbingly, is there a difference and where is it?

The culture defines the first moment of a woman's sexual experience as making the difference between girl and woman. A typological model allows the Aesthetics to equate a virgin from myth, Andromeda or Princess Sabra in the St. George myth or Angelica from Ariosto's romance, for example, and the Virgin Mary herself. Then they subvert the distinction between chaste and unchaste women. By focusing on the moment of the physical act separating maiden from woman, they probe the concept of chastity to expose its paradoxes. What, they ask, has essentially changed? Angelica's and Mary's moment of defloration is the Aesthetics' typological moment.

Typological moments depend upon a concept of historical time, the fulfillment redeeming the prefigurement of an earlier moment. The typology of sexuality in Rossetti demarcates an individual's identity by an analogous process. Typological fulfillment becomes for them also sexual fulfillment, as spiritual lily also symbolizes defloration. Defloration involves a moment of merging in which man and woman come together, merging genders as well as bodies. Aesthetic typology does not resolve the problem of sexual difference but rather serves to represent it as a problem. Rossetti, Morris, and Burne-Jones employ the Virgin of the Annunciation and Andromeda of the Rock to question traditional distinctions—not only the oppositions between body and soul, sacred and profane but also an equally fundamental and equally unsettling distinction between male and female.

By focusing on the moment of female defloration, the Aesthetics express an anxious interest in female sexuality. They imagine the rescue scene as the loss of female virginity, but express an uneasy curiosity about what precisely happens during that definitive event. The supposedly fearless hero "rescues" the virgin, paradoxically by making her a non-virgin. But what about him? In the problematic of that rescue what happens to maleness as well as to femaleness?

Pater provides an aesthetic vocabulary to explore such questions. As opposed to Buchanan's rejection of the Aesthetics' dangerous typology, he was sympathetic to their techniques, describing how his contemporaries filtered myth through Christian heroic stories, mediating pagan values with the morality of intervening history, a process that Erwin Panofsky has usefully termed "pseudomorphosis" in regard to the Renaissance classical revival.[13] In tracing the typological pedigree of the group, Pater recognized that all artistic creations occur "in mixed lights and in mixed situations."[14] Despite the mixing of past and present and the limitations placed upon an artist in revivals of established narratives, Pater discerned in any recounting of any myth the indelible stamp of a present moment. Literary revivals, like architectural or decorative reproductions, alter the past with unmistakable contemporary lineaments. The Aesthetics tried to erase signs of temporality by filtering their particular moment through a distancing light. Past and present merged, producing an illusion of timelessness, untainted by specific historical events.

Pater suggested that the Aesthetics fulfilled a type, prefigured in the cloisters of the Middle Ages. In an 1868 review essay on the poetry of William Morris, later retitled "Aesthetic Poetry," he described the process of change that interpretation gives to a story as it passes through historical time. "For us," Pater confessed, including his own sensibility with that of Morris and Rossetti, "the most attractive story is the monk's conception of it, when he escapes from the sombre legend of his cloister to that true (or, as he later revised it, "natural") light."[15] Pater's monk emerges into a light bearing a complicated relation to Wordsworth's light of common day. It is a light influenced by Romanticism, natural as the saturated light before a hurricane. The revival of myth has a hybrid quality, resulting from intervening cultural developments. Paradoxically, because of its fleshly truth, the monk who could best recount the myth could not best understand it. His cloistered spirituality blocks him from the myth's meaning, but the mixed light of his story casts upon the tale an essential coloration of the cloister, giving the story sanctity or, in one of Rossetti's favorite words, "mystery." According to Pater, this is the version of classical myth that the Aesthetics prefer—one that makes available more than a cloistered monk could allow himself to know and conveys what he could not:

> The fruits of this mood, which, divining more than it understands, infuses into the figures of the Christian legend some subtle reminiscence of older gods, or into the story of Cupid and Psyche that passionate stress of spirit which the world owes to Christianity, have still to be gathered up when the time comes.[16]

Pater claims that his own aesthetic company restored Christian versions of classical myths to their true meaning.

Pater's revisionary Aesthetics arrived typologically at the proper moment to gather in the truth couched in medievalized myths. "Truth" could be discerned in the Andromeda myth, for example, by those Aesthetic initiates who received sanction for their synthesizing double vision from earlier mythographers. Pater's revision imitates Pauline typology only to undermine it, first claiming that Christianity inadequately understood antiquity and then finding both pagan and Christian tradition equally incomplete. He does what typologists have always done—claimed that those earlier in the progression were unwilling signifiers rather than comprehenders of signification. It is his group who can fulfill the promise of the earlier myths. Pater, who was engaged in a similar project, recognized the Aesthetics' typological means of transposing from antiquity to Christianity and from Christianity to pagan myth to discover adequate representations for their own concerns about gender and sexuality.

By cloaking Andromeda's story in venerable garb, the Aesthetics filter their earthly concerns through the colored windows of the cloister and the timeless mists of classical myth. Whereas the monk's typological method would privilege the Christian view as a fulfillment of the shadowy pagan and Hebrew types, the Aesthetics equate Christian and antique. Both earlier stories tell the same amorous message about a sexual encounter, ritualized and symbolized. The language of typology thus points to literal meaning. "Fulfillment," which to the Church Fathers signified the new dispensation, has become reincarnated, made once again fleshly and overtly sexual. In the Aesthetics' representation, Andromeda is fulfilled sexually by being rescued; the hero who drops from the sky, like the dove, brings to her a "message" that gives her life meaning.

That these late Victorians so elaborately figured sexuality in this way is itself a measure of their preoccupation and repression that leads us to label such attitudes toward sexuality as "Victorian." The relations between the sexes, a social arrangement, becomes sexualized, the social construct symbolized in the sexual act. Sexual activity is symbolic of gender relations. The question about virginity—a question about gender as well as about sex—

raises questions for the Aesthetics about the power relations symbolized by sexual intercourse.

Fleshly Annunciations

PATER LABELED Dante Gabriel Rossetti's symbolic method "an insanity of realism,"[17] capturing nicely the poet's ability to imbue small details with preternatural meaning. Under the stress of a charged moment, realistic detail becomes more than distinct and reaches beyond what reality ordinarily can bear. Caught in the midst of this moment, intensity turns into potential or even momentary instanity. Pater observed that for Rossetti, "life is a crisis at every moment."[18] In the sense that a crisis is a decisive turning point, distinguishing irrevocably the past from the present, like the Annunciation, the moment of Andromeda's rescue is such a crisis. Rossetti's topology makes an ordinary moment, one that any girl might experience, into a sacramental moment. Mary's story recounts a virgin's encounter with the mystery of sexuality. In turn, Mary's story is parallel to Eve's encounter with the serpent in the Garden of Eden. The teller of these women's stories, a man full of anxious questions about what is happening, interprets all the stories typologically to represent the same moment of intense desire.

During the same years that he wrote his two sonnets on Ruggiero rescuing Angelica, Rossetti, also meditated on the early life of the Virgin Mary.[19] The title of his first major oil, *The Girlhood of Mary Virgin* (1848–49, figure 3.1) emphasizes by its verbal inversion not only a characteristic archaizing but also the word "virgin." Dante Gabriel knew that he was interested in Mary specifically as a girl. In 1852 he wrote to F. G. Stephens, making a nice distinction between stages in a woman's life: "That picture of mine was a symbol of female excellence. The Virgin being taken as its highest type. It was not her *Childhood* but her *Girlhood*."[20] Rossetti specifies a type of untouched virginal female perfection denoted by "girl."

Rossetti's painting deploys the characters in spaces appropriate to the Victorian convention of the separate spheres for men and

3.1. Dante Gabriel Rossetti, *The Girlhood of Mary Virgin*
Reproduced with permission of the Tate Gallery, London.

women. The women in the painting work inside, mother teaching daughter how to embroider, and father works outside, tending a vine. Lack of depth telescopes the two spheres at once confirming and denying the convention. Separating the spheres of man and woman but then conflating them is analogous to the Aesthetics' androgynous imagery. In his metaphysics of gender, the lily plays a significant symbolic role. In this painting, Mary sews a copy of the plant tended by an angel. The flower becomes the symbolic center of the Aesthetic typology of defloration.

Rossetti builds upon the elements suggested by his painting in poems written during the same period of time. He wrote a series of ekphrastic sonnets, collected as "Sonnets on Pictures" and writen mainly between 1847 and 1850, the years of his interest in the Virgin Mary. Two works from that series, the first on an Annunciation painting Rossetti discovered in an auction room and the other a double sonnet on Ingres' *Ruggiero délivrant Angelica,* a painting he had seen in the Louvre, employ a sacred typological vocabulary to symbolize defloration. In "For an Annunciation, Early German" (1845?) Rossetti makes the time distinction essential for typological interpretation. The Incarnation marks the dividing line between shadowy type and fulfillment, between fallen time and time redeemed. The poem captures the instant in time of that miracle:

> She was Faith's Present, parting what had been
> From what began with her, and is for aye.
> On either hand, God's twofold system lay:
> With meek bowed face a Virgin prayed between.
> (p. 343)

The Virgin's physical movement acts out the symbolic moment as she turns after the dove flies in to her:

> So prays she, and the Dove flies in to her,
> And she has turned.
> (ll. 9–10)

As a Virgin's (not "the" Virgin) flesh stands between God's twofold system, her physical movement acts out the turning point that the particular act of annunciation represents. Her action turns an act of language—an announcement—into an act of flesh. The landscape intensifies the reciprocal sexual suggestion of the Dove's movement in to her and her turning toward it. The Virgin's lilies yield to the pressure of the Dove's flight in a meeting and merging of the Virgin's porch with the natural world that it reproduces or doubles:

> Heavy with heat, the plants yield shadow there;
> The loud flies cross each other in the sun;
> And the aisled pillars meet the poplar-aisle.
> (ll. 12–14)

The distinction between a religious moment sexualized and a sexual moment spiritualized collapse in the poem. The flies cross each other in an imitation of prayer that may also constitute a sexual meeting; the alternations of sound in the last line flank and emphasize the verb "meet," for the poem is about the holiness of the physical meeting in which history turns from one kind of time to another. A private moment, enacted in natural light by the meanest creatures, marks the revolutionary change to Christian time. Pater describes Rossetti's landscapes as being incorporated into, not simply added to, the human event: "lifeless nature is translated into a higher service in which it does but incorporate itself with some phase of strong emotion."[21] This annunciation preserves a virgin's passivity and purity because the landscape and the language substitute for her actions. In their heat the lilies—Mary's plants—yield; the flies loudly cross; the natural poplars and the pillars—their created mirror—come together.

Ecce Ancilla Domini (1850; figure 3.2), Rossetti's most familiar annunciation painting, contains suggestions of the more overt sexual symbolism in the Ruggiero and Angelica sonnets. The painting also reflects the gender ambiguity of many other Aesthetic representations. Rossetti manipulates the convention of the reluctant virgin where Mary seems to ward off the announcement of the honor she is about to receive. The cowering virgin retreats as the angel Gabriel advances. The painting describes a meeting of a physical man and a physical woman. Rossetti added Gabriel's halo after the painting was sold;[22] without the halos and the flames under Gabriel's feet, the two figures seem self-conscious young people in a rather awkward intimate meeting. The peculiar perspective emphasizes intimacy, pushing the figures more to the front than most Pre-Raphaelite paintings. As in *The Girlhood of Mary Virgin,* the scene thrusts toward the viewer because of the perspective in which Mary seems to be tipping out of a bed that is too small as she retreats from the advancing flower stem upon which her eyes are fixed. The physical intimacy is precisely the point: whatever is spiritual happens literally in a fleshly encounter. Furthermore, the androgynous figures, both dressed identically, seem almost to encounter themselves. Although the angel Gabriel looks older and more powerful than the Virgin Mary, he does not look identifiably masculine. The lily and the tiny dove perching above the top blossom are the instruments of conception.[23]

William Michael Rossetti self-consciously defended what might have appeared too homely about the scene: ". . . the Virgin is to be in bed, but without any bedclothes on, an arrangement which may be justified in consideration of the hot climate, and the Angel Gabriel is to be presenting a lily to her."[24] The stem of the flower points to the finished flower embroidery Mary was working on in Rossetti's picture of her girlhood. The lily embroidery prefigured the fulfillment of this moment, the instrument of conception and its symbolic representation coming together, fulfilling the promise.

A similarly torrid climate heats the atmosphere in "Ave," a long poem rewritten about the same time. As in the sonnet for the early German painting, the characters are arrested, seemingly motionless; the landscape expresses their passion. The poem opens after Mary has been translated to Heaven, and the speaker addresses her as "wife unto the Holy Ghost"; he then meditates on the moment of the annunciation "when June's heavy breath/ Warmed the long days in Nazareth" (p. 244).[25] Thoughts about the climate, personified by June's desire, breathing heavily, identify the month with the divine spirit or breath, panting during a fraught physical moment. The landscape expresses the physical encounter and the feeling attached to it:

DGR
March 1850

> Far off the trees were as pale wands
> Against the fervid sky: the sea
> Sighed further off eternally
> As human sorrow sighs in sleep.
> Then suddenly the awe grew deep . . .
> (p. 244)

The sea bears the weight of a sorrow that is not only specifically human but is an ordinary domestic event, as common as a sleeper's sigh. The sorrow is unconscious, expressed only in sleep, such as in the bedroom of *Ecce Ancilla Domini,* where the Virgin seems startled into an upright position on her bed, almost in the trance-like state of one who is not yet fully awake. The sea sighs as if in anticipation for the loss that is yet an essential component of eternal Christian joy.

Like Rossetti's sonnets on the German Annunciation, "For Ruggiero and Angelica by Ingres" (figure 3.3) describes a sexual encounter. Rossetti's double sonnet on the Ingres painting presents Angelica's moment—like the Virgin Mary's—as a specifically sexual turning point, focused on a similarly confined woman. Whereas the Annunciation landscape expressed the passion of the charged moment, the dragon slaying conveys a stronger sense of the violence of defloration. Rather than diffuse its sexual aggression in the landscape, Rossetti transfers it to the dragon slaying. He imagines Angelica's annunciation from the maiden's point of view as a sexual crisis, a moment separating virgin from non-virgin. The passage from one state to the other—which he makes religious by using the word "anoints"—is dangerous, not only for the woman but for the man as well.[26]

Ingres' painting spiritualizes the more lusty Ariosto, arresting the characters in romantic attitudes. Ruggiero rides a griffin, an elaboration of the more stalwart Pegasus. Angelica assumes a languorous pose, tilting her head backwards at an extreme angle, distorting her neck into a shape that contemporary critics derided as a third breast. Rossetti mentions "the throat let back" in his

3.2. Dante Gabriel Rossetti, *Ecce Ancilla Domini*
Reproduced with permission of the Tate Gallery, London.

first sonnet; as a motif in Aesthetic renditions, this throat becomes the dragon's neck, held back at a similar angle. Ruggiero's enormous pike divides the canvas, giving this somewhat static painting its major movement. This pike, like the stem of the lily, becomes eroticized in other Aesthetic representations. It is a symbol

3.3. Jean Dominique Ingres, *Ruggiero délivrant Angelica*
Reproduced by permission of the National Gallery, London.

of domination, a counterpart to the tall, narrow rock to which Angelica is chained.

The sea and sky of the opening line of Rossetti's ekphrastic sonnet connect this mythological scene to the imagined sea and the fervid sky of "Ave": "A remote sky, prolonged to the sea's brim" (p. 347). By virtue of the word "brim," as if the sea were a large bowl, like a baptismal font, the sky's remoteness evokes the impersonality of ritual rather than a distant, vast nothingness. Again, the landscape participates in the scene. In the sestet Rossetti deepens and reinforces the ritual suggestions of the octave. The sky is "harsh and the sea shrewd and salt," the word "shrewd" in this context indicating not only harsh and dangerous but knowing.

The moment occurs on a significant boundary between earth and water, emphasized by the "one rock point," a marginal setting with the rock mediating between the elements of sea and water, a traditional dwelling place for monsters. The monster is the product of an unnatural birth: "a foul beast unknown,/Hell-birth of geomaunt and teraphim" (I, ll. 3–4). The archaic words are not merely stunners; they both refer to the art of divination, in the first by means of signs derived from handsful of earth, in the second by means of household gods.[27] In both words the gender is unclear, and the unholy union of the two produces a "hell-birth." The coupling of geomaunt and terraphim produces the monster, monstrously prefiguring the sexual act described in the sonnets.

In the midst of the nonhuman forces, the fettered, naked woman's flesh shines forth, her loose hair contrasting with her still body. Rossetti takes his interpretation partly from Ariosto, who copies Ovid's comparison of the woman to the rock. Women, particularly beautiful and naked ones, are made by men from rocks similar to those to which this woman is chained:

> Her would Rogero have some statue demed
> Of alabaster made, or marble rare,
> Which to the rock so fastened seemed
> By the industrious sculptor's cunning care,

> But that he saw distinct a tear which streamed
> Amid fresh opening rose and lily fair,
> Stand on her budding paps beneath in dew,
> And that her golden hair disheveled flew.[28]

Except for her hair, Angelica seems a part of the rock; her tears turn into landscape as dew on the flowers that are her breasts. Rossetti also confounds the difference between human and nature's moistures. To reinforce the impression of Angelica merged with the landscape, Rossetti's griffin and knight halt before the rock, as if the naked marble-like woman were inorganic: "A knight, and a winged creature bearing him,/ Reared at the rock." Ingres' griffin seems to brake at the moment before crashing into the rock, its claws spread and bracing. The painter's Ruggiero focuses his gaze on the dragon, but the poet turns the important encounter to one between the man and the woman, emphasizing their gender, turning the battle into a symbol of an erotic meeting.

The first sonnet describes the meeting represented in the painting, interpreting it as a judgment about sexuality. The speaker's voice echoes Pater's imaginary monk, coloring the moment with a moral tone: "The sky is harsh" (I, 9). Rossetti turns the scene into a moment of knowledge, drawing not only from Ariosto and Ingres but also from the Bible:

> The spear's lithe stem
> Thrills in the roaring of those jaws: behind,
> That evil length of body chafes at fault.
> She does not hear nor see—she knows of them.
> (I. 11–14)

Angelica knows both about the rescuing hero and the evil length of body. Like the spirit woman her name implies, she knows what is happening but is senseless. Until the monster dies she may not be innocent or without shame, but she lacks some essential quality, a kind of full consciousness.

The griffin horse "ramping and rigid" enacts sexual excitement as the "spear's lithe stem" enters the jaws of the unknown foul beast. The spear's stem replaces the lily's stem of the German Annunciation, the same word indicating a parallel deflowering. Rossetti explores more explicitly the negative and fearful elements of the sexual encounter than he has in the Annunciation poems. Using typological time, he defines the moment before the "slaying" as the "last instant," the moment separating one kind of time from another. By asking questions of this moment without answering them, he makes a mystery of sexuality—a technique Yeats employed in a similar moment in "Leda and the Swan." He asks, what made her wet?:

> Was that the scattered whirl
> Of its foam drenched thee:—or the waves that curl
> And split, bleak spray wherein thy temples ache?
> Or was it his the champion's blood to flake
> Thy flesh?—or thine own blood's anointing, girl?
>
> (II. 4–8)

The sexual import gives both a religious and anatomical meaning to "temples." In this temple a ritual anointing occurs, involving, like the mass, a blood sacrifice. Not the savior's, this blood suggests woman's defloration, its source difficult to discern in the moment of merging. The speaker continues to question. If it is blood and not ocean spray, whose blood is it—the champion's or her own—that assures the girl's passage into knowledge? The repetition of "girl" in the octave of the second sonnet suggests that a transformation from girl to woman occurs in the moment of anointing. The monster's dying, a climax that arrests time, is verbally suggeted by the repetition of "now" in the first three lines of the sestet:

> Now silence: for the sea's is such a sound
> As irks not silence; and except the sea,
> All now is still. Now the dead thing doth cease
> To writhe and drifts He turns to her
>
> (II. 9–12).

Rosetti uses the same turning gesture at the same typological moment as in the Annunciation sonnet, but he rather than she moves.

Saved from death (in her "dying"), but still bound, she is restored: "Again a woman in her nakedness" (II. 14). At the moment of consummation she is neither girl nor woman but a merged being. The boundaries and distinctions between man and woman have become irrelevant during the moment when time stops and distinctions blur. The long stem enters unknown regions of the creature who makes an unearthly sound. Separated from the act, Angelica—her name reflecting her idealized being—knows what is happening but is senseless—mind without body.

Couching mysterious knowledge in her body, Angelica is a type of Eve at the moment of sexual initiation. Slaying or calming "the thing" gives her carnal knowledge. Like Eve, Angelica has fallen, and, as in Rossetti's Annunciation sonnet, the fleshly moment separates one kind of time from another. The last line, "Again a woman in her nakedness" restores the anxious man to a kind of knowledge too. He sees her and knows that she is Woman.

Rossetti turns the Virgin's and the Maiden's story into an amorous one. He designed a stained-glass window of St. George and the Dragon which also turns the saint's legend into a strangely but equally sexual one (figure 3.4). The legend gives the Princess an even more peripheral role than the Greek myth, but this marginality foregrounds and further emphasizes the multiple significations of monster slaying. From one perspective, saint, monster, and maiden enact an eternal triangle, defined by Eve Sedgwick as "homosocial" desire, the real engagement between the two males.[29] For that interaction, the monster is male and the battle between the two males for her masks their valuation of each other. From another perspective, the battle between monster and hero is a symbolic counterpart of sexual intercourse. For that encounter, the monster is female. The supernatural struggle between saint and monster transfers the sexual act between man and woman to the dragon slaying.

St. George usually slays his adversary at the relatively comfortable distance of a long spear or sword. In this design, however, the saint kneels with his arm in the dragon's mouth as he plunges a sword into its midriff. The dragon embraces the saint, his coils encircling St. George's body, the scaly tail ends in an arrowhead-like shape at the saint's crotch, suggestively phallic.

The embrace, aggressive limb in orifice, suggests the sexual act but separates the princess from it. When she appears at all in conventional depictions, the princess is fully clothed, but in Rossetti's design her bare arms, bound together, hang over her drooping head. Her dress slides off to her waist exposing her breasts, a departure from convention that emphasizes a sexuality redolent of torment. Here, Rossetti turns rescue into orgy.

Aesthetic typology suggests that the three maidens—Mary, Andromeda, Princess Sabra—express not simply the male's fleshly desire for the maiden but his fear of her as well. Freud describes this combination of attraction and terror in his discussion of the taboo of virginity.[30] The taboo occurs because the power of the virgin requires a ritual of defloration of the Virgin Bride by some-

3.4. Dante Gabriel Rossetti, "St. George," design for stained glass window
Reproduced by permission of the City of Birmingham Museums and Art Gallery.

one other than the groom. As Rossetti limns the German Annunciation, he describes Gabriel as "one" who looks on as the dove flies in to Mary, as if the Holy Ghost were protecting Gabriel from the taboo of virginity. Similar rituals are suggested in Ruggiero's thrill of the spear's stem and in Gabriel's proferring of the lily's stem, both of which are phallic substitutions. In the mythological version the monster merges male and female characteristics: its roaring jaws the female, its writhing length of body the male. The intimacy between St. George and the dragon also suggests sexual symbolism. Substituting monster for maiden, the male limb enters into the monster's head. *The Wedding of St. George and Princess Sabra* (1857, figure 3.5) contains a correlative to the typology of defloration. In the lower right corner, prominently foregrounded, a bizarre monster's head thrusts upward out of a box. The monster in the "box" is an icon for the moment of merging, possessing both sexes, like a hermaphrodite. The angle of the detached head parodies Angelica's throat let back, while huge teeth in the monster's open mouth make explicit the dangers, now linked to erotic risks. The monster box safely contains all monstrous sexual possibilities, separating them from the loving couple who are its saintly counterparts, now legitimately wedded.

Domesticated Annunciations

ROSETTI'S DISCIPLES, William Morris and Edward Burne-Jones, echo and adapt Rossetti's questions about female virginity and male anxiety, not only in their treatments of the Perseus and Andromeda myth but also in their amalgamation of Arthurian, Christian, and classical symbolism. The close association between Rossetti, Morris, and Burne-Jones, beginning in 1856 when the younger men discovered Pre-Raphaelite paintings, clearly emerges in their similar typological iconography, connecting Andromeda, Virgin Mary, and Eve. In his appreciation of Morris' use of Arthurian legend, Pater describes the rationale for drawing typological parallels among the three stories:

> These Arthurian legends, pre-Christian in their origin, yield all their sweetness only in a Christian atmosphere. What is char-

> acteristic in them is the strange suggestion of a deliberate choice between Christ and rival lover . . . The jealousy of that other lover, for whom these words and images and strange ways of sentiment were first devised, is the secret here of a triumphant color and heat. Who knows whether, when the simple belief in them has faded away, the most cherished sacred writing may not for the first time exercise their highest influence as the most delicate amorous poetry in the world.[31]

The sweet meaning of both Christian and Arthurian legends derives from their competing significations which Aesthetic typol-

3.5. Dante Gabriel Rossetti, *The Wedding of St. George and Princess Sabra*
Reproduced by permission of the Tate Gallery, London.

ogy interprets amorously. The figurations of Morris and Burne-Jones elaborate upon Rossetti's annunciation-romance.

Pater's insight that Morris uses the iconography of Christian stories to give a sacred aura to Arthurian legend applies to Guenevere's profane and immoral behavior in "The Defence of Guenevere." As Morris structures it, Guenevere's explanation of her adultery draws upon the iconography of Annunciation paintings. The scene is a bedroom, but rather than sexual consummation being an expected outcome, it is depicted as an unpredictable visitation. Guenevere describes her encounter with Launcelot as if it were an Annunciation. Imagine, she asks her accusers, that you are on your death bed, and you have a vision. How can you know whether the vision was heaven or hell sent?:

"Suppose a hush should come, then some one speak:

" 'One of these cloths is heaven, and one is hell,
Now choose one cloth for ever; which they be,
I will not tell you, you must somehow tell

" 'Of your own strength and mightiness; here, see!'
Yea, yea, my lord, and you to ope your eyes,
At foot of your familiar bed to see

"A great God's angel standing, with such dyes,
Not known on earth, on his great wings, and hands,
Held out two ways, light from the inner skies

"Showing him well, and making his commands
Seem to be God's commands, moreover, too,
Holding within his hands the cloths on wands;

"And one of these strange choosing cloths was blue,
Wavy and long, one cut short and red;
No man could tell the better of the two.

"After shivering half-hour you said:
'God help! heaven's colour, the blue;" and he said: 'hell.'[32]

Guenevere conflates death and annunciation as she describes a scene, similar to Rossetti's painting, the Virgin in bed with Gabriel standing at the foot of her bed. Morris draws upon one doctrinal sense, of the Annunciation as a death scene. The Hail Mary destroyed the Virgin's past even as it was supposedly her most pleasurable moment, signalling the death of the past with the beginning of a new historical era. In Guenevere's revision Launcelot is the angel Gabriel; like Mary, she is married. Rather than an angel her vision is a monstrous apparition. In her defense nothing is what is should be. By all odds Guenevere's choice of the more attractive blue cloth would be correct. It is wavy and long, like virginal hair, while the red one is "cut short," deliberately truncated, not simply naturally short. Furthermore, the blue color of heaven, the virgin's color, implicitly allies the cloth (and perhaps Guenevere as well in choosing it) with the Virgin. But Guenevere's manipulation of symbols marks her modern sensibility; she knows that typological allegory is arbitrary, that the world may not shadow a greater reality. She plays with a capricious semiotic universe.

Yet Morris' Guenevere shares some of the Virgin's attributes and, like Andromeda, she is rescued. What is announced as a triumph and a rescue, however, may be something else; Morris and Burne-Jones cast doubt on the value of rescue by the way they construct the typological moment. In their subsequent representations of the Perseus and Andromeda myth the trinity of monster, man, and woman is so fractured that the myth expresses the fears, terrors, and desires lurking behind the archetypal Victorian image of rescuing knight and bound, virtuous lady. By including the story of Perseus and Medusa, Morris and Burne-Jones bring to the foreground the dangerous relationship of monsters and humans.

Morris develops the sexual dimension of rescue in his version of the Perseus legend in *The Earthly Paradise.* He retells the Perseus legend as part of a narrative cycle, framing it with a medieval setting. During the Black Death people from different parts of the globe left their land in fear to discover among the unexplored Western seas an Earthly Paradise where there was no sickness, old age, or death. Although they fail in their quest, old age finds them settled on an island where the people speak ancient Greek. They celebrate their placid old age by telling two stories, one by a Greek, the other by a Wanderer.

For April, the Greek narrative is "The Doom of Acrisius," the story of Perseus, grandson of Acrisius and the executor of his doom. As the torrid Levantine climate infuses Rossetti's annunciations with sexuality, so Morris' April climate symbolizes the sexual ambiguities of his story. Before presenting the myth, Morris distills its significance as similar to April's multiple identities. April is "midspring"—a bittersweet moment, precisely because it merges opposites:

> Ah! life of all the year, why yet do I
> Amid thy snowy blossoms' fragrant drift
> Still long for that which never draweth night,
> Striving my pleasure from my pain to sift,
> Some weight from off my fluttering mirth to lift?
> —Now, when far bells are ringing, "Come again,
> Come back, past years! why will ye pass in vain!"[33]

Morris imagines opposites as being enmeshed, as in the "snowy blossoms" which conflate the seasons. Similarly pain and pleasure merge inextricably as the melancholy speaker sets himself the impossible task of sifting one from the other. Temporally, too, the speaker stands between a vanished past and an unattainable future. April also becomes a sign of the border between types of women—maiden and seductress—one passively drawing down the active male and the other actively destroying the petrified male. Morris balances the pleasures of sexual love with a virgin Andromeda against the sexual pains inflicted by her opposite or double, Medusa.[34]

Morris' Perseus poises between two women—his mother and his eventual wife. The third woman—supernatural and dangerous—must be slain in order for him to attain full masculinity, to move, that is, from mother to wife. He is helped in this task by Minerva, a virgin goddess who rejects maternal for patriarchal law and bears great rage against the beautiful Medusa. Perseus' fate is thus determined by women. Through them he achieves proper masculine identity. Morris gives all the women a voice, allowing them to explain their feelings, but eventually all those feelings ultimately give the young man his rightful and heroic place in history.

Morris' social consciousness of women's market value is implicit in his depiction of women's hair; he evaluates all the important women in the hero's life by the quality of their hair, either alluring or repelling.[35] King Polydectes sends Perseus off to slay Medusa, whose hair is part of her legendary horror, because the King is enflamed with desire at the sight of Danaë's "yellow hair,/ Wreathed round with olive wreaths, that hung adown/ Over the soft folds of her linen gown" (p. 190). The repellent women in the myth have loathsome or lank hair, while the desirable women have magnificent hair. Morris describes the Graiae and the landscape they inhabit as devoid of color—all white: a bare white marble wall with milk-white pillars, snow-white gowns "While o'er their backs their straight white hair hung down/ In long thin locks; dreadful their faces were" (p. 199).

Perseus passes from this white world of sexual decay, symbolized by the one eye the Graiae are condemned to share, to the more frightening Gorgon world, where the landscape is leaden: a "black and shining wall" encloses the pathetic but dangerous Medusa. Morris emphasizes the Gorgon's victimization by Neptune's rape and Minerva's punishment. In her rape and imprisonment, the Medusa mirrors Danaë, who was imprisoned first and then violated. In a departure from convention, Medusa's golden hair has not been transformed into the snakes of the phallic woman. Rather the phallic snakes have invaded her golden hair, both her value and her shame. Medusa paces in her prison, moaning and shrieking:

> Because the golden tresses of her hair
> Were moved by writhing snakes from side to side
> That in their writhing oftentimes would glide
> On to her breast, or shuddering shoulder white;
> (p. 203)

The snakes perpetually reenact her rape, her transformation from a virtuous maiden to an alluring monster. Medusa's memories of her virginal times include "flowery meadows," "song of birds, rustle of the trees," and "the prattle of the children." These recollections of a happier innocent past resemble the meditations of a Romantic poet. Medusa's condition suggests what could happen to a Wordsworthian poet were he a woman. Like the Romantic poet, she remembers her childhood moral development in the company of nature, but unlike the male poet, her youthful memories are not recollected in tranquillity but in Gothic torture.

For Morris, Medusa's slaying not only fulfills Perseus' duty to his mother, who will be unprotected unless he returns, but is a heroic act of mercy. Jerome J. McGann formulates this central romantic event as an act of love. "Perseus is for Morris, Medusa's first real lover," he claims, "who, instead of raping her with a cruel selfishness, like Neptune, kills her out of a wonderful love."[36] The terms of the myth seem to allow no alternatives for the object of male desire. The real act of love here is decapitation, truly monstrous. Morris portrays this act of sympathetic murder as euthanasia, a sort of rescue and an act of love with no alternative but rape. Medusa's power—always and forever to petrify men, leading them to acts of violence—is indeed a hateful burden for her only to be relieved by a horrible death. Perseus "loves" Medusa aggressively, whereas he transfers the aggression of his love for Andromeda to slaying a monster.

Medusa resembles both Danaë, Perseus' mother, and Andromeda, his eventual bride. She, too, is imprisoned in a fortress like the one Danaë's father built to contain his daughter, but Medusa's is of natural rock, like the one to which Andromeda is tied. All three women are not only deprived of free movement because of female sexuality, but their imprisonment is symbolic of how sexuality confines women. They are bound by the law of the father whose stone fortress, whether it be man-made or natural, limits them.

Both raped by a god, Danaë and Medusa are defined as fallen women and banished. Andromeda, too, is banished by her people, but she is blameless. Paralleling the action of his father, her hero falls miraculously through the air, as did Zeus to Danaë, but, unlike a god, he comes not to rape but to rescue the victimized woman. In typological terms the son of Zeus redeems the rape of his mother first by reenacting his father's descent from the sky, but instead of raping and abandoning his victim, he marries her. Andromeda's sexual attractiveness resembles the two other women's, but she is an appropriate mate for Perseus. He may make love to her, which he begins to do before he kills the dragon, her would-be ravager. The three women's stories operate paratactically in Morris' narrative, commenting on each other. Morris' Perseus battles to constitute, or to "rescue" the safely feminine, that constructed gender essential for dynastic ambition. Made virginal, the woman in peril can be made into a wife.[37]

Unlike Medusa, the golden-haired Andromeda cannot even pace because her chains confine her. Perseus arrives on this scene before the ravishing, not by Neptune this time but by a grotesque emissary sent by the sea god. Andromeda draws the hero out of the sky with her cries. Morris describes the bronze of the maiden's chains as parodies of her golden hair:

> Naked except for the tresses of her hair
> That o'er her white limbs by the breeze were wound,
> And brazen chains her weary arms that bound
> Unto the sea-beat overhanging rock,
> As though her golden-crowned head to mock.
>
> (p. 210)

By comparing hair and chains as Andromeda's only attire, Morris suggests that the attraction of woman is her available sexuality and her helplessness. Gold hair chains the woman whom it crowns.

Melting with the same pity he felt for Medusa, Perseus is also inflamed with love:

> And grey eyes glittering with his great desire
> Beneath his hair, that like a harmless fire
> Blown by the wind shone in her hopeless eyes.
>
> (p. 211)

The pupils of Andromeda's eyes reflect Perseus' noble and therefore harmless desire. Reflection mutes danger, dramatically echoing the proscription against gazing directly at Medusa.

Andromeda's eyes, like a mirror, simply reflect Perseus' desire, expressing no desire of their own. The words "harmless" and "hopeless" oppose each other in tense negation. For Andromeda there is hope as long as Perseus is harmless. The Medusa's eyes cannot be met because they represent the ultimately harmful desire of women. The meeting of eyes between Andromeda and Perseus is a charm against the other, the Medusan meeting, in which passion may be the woman's as well as the man's—or, worse, may be hers alone. Since the taking of Andromeda is imagined as a rescue, her only desire is to be saved. She has no other desire of her own, and so she reflects perfectly that of her liberator who otherwise would be petrified.

As the two speak and Andromeda bewails her fate, Perseus frees her from her chains. The sea monster draws nigh. The maiden begs for one last kiss before being devoured by the monster. As Perseus kisses her he sees the monster through the strands of her hair:

> He came to her and kissed her as she sank
> Into his arms, and from the horror shrank
> Clinging to him, scarce knowing he was there;
> But through the drifting wonder of her hair,
> Amidst his pity, he beheld the sea,
> And saw a huge wave rising mightily
> Above the smaller breakers of the shore,
> Which in its green breast for a minute bore
> A nameless horror, that it cast alond
> And left, a huge mass on the oozing sand,
> That scarcely seemed a living thing to be,
>
> (p. 214)

Andromeda's drifting hair forms a blind, through which Perseus espies the monster. Her hair forms a "hair tent" prized by Victorian poets, a protection which makes dangerous visions possible.[38] Through the filtering hair, Perseus beholds a nameless horror, a huge mass, scarcely living. Although the primitive beast is masculine, it is also parallel to the female Gorgon Medusa. Perseus treats it similarly. He lops off its head, bringing it as a gift to lay at Andromeda's feet. After hearing of her rescuer's exploits, the maiden begs to view the Medusa's head:

> "This salt pool nigh
> Left by the tide, now mirrors well the sky,
> So smooth it is, and now I stand anear
> Canst thou not see my foolish visage clear,
> Yea, e'en the little gems upon my hands?
> May I not see this marvel of the lands
> So mirrored, and yet live?
>
> (pp. 216–17)

Andromeda implicitly compares her own face and jeweled hands reflected in the calm of the sea with what she wants to look at. Medusa and Andromeda are thus "reflections" of each other. But Andromeda, a good girl, knows enough to deprecate her own face. Her "foolish visage," she implies, cannot harm anyone. Unlike the Medusa's it is unknowing, "foolish." It cannot contain petrifying plots but can only reflect male desire. So mirrored and weakened, Medusan desire can be looked at since the love of Andromeda and Perseus tames monstrous desires. The grotesque male and more horrible female have been decapitated; love domesticates the unbound lust they represent. Andromeda can gaze upon her reflected double; Perseus can bring the head of the "slimy loathsome coil" to the woman he loves and can expect her to admire it.

Morris and Burne-Jones embellish Rossetti's story. They grapple with his questions about what happens when a man deflowers a virgin. What happens after the Fall? Whereas the Christian story transfers the danger of transgression and the burden of salvation to the deity's son, the classical myth preserves the danger, not in an offspring but in monsters.

Burne-Jones preserves suggestions of the typological system connecting the Annunciation to the Andromeda legend. In his handling of the St. George legend and in his series of paintings of the Perseus and Andromeda legend, he explores the dangers of both male and female sexuality, and, at the same time, submerges the threat in the curiously androgynous figures which appear to deny the danger by calming, absorbing, or domesticating it.[39]

Burne-Jones developed as an artist under the discipleship of Rossetti, who acted as mentor, and Morris, a classmate at Oxford, who provided funds and ideas. While Burne-Jones was living with Morris in Red Lion Square and seeing Rossetti daily, he designed a stained-glass window of the Annunciation which brought him criticism similar to that leveled by Buchanan at Rossetti. In 1860 he designed three windows for St. Columba's church in Topcliffe, Yorkshire, but the architect found that Burne-Jones' Virgin Mary clasped the dove to her breast too ardently, a sacrilege that lost the artist his commission.[40] A drawing of the annunciation of the same year recalls the vertical style of *Ecce Ancilla Domini*. Burne-Jones' similarly fleshly depictions of the annunciation, his many paintings of St. George, and his Perseus series were incubated in the intimacy of the Aesthetic School. He undertook to illustrate *The Earthly Paradise,* and, although he did not complete the project, the iconography of the Perseus and Andromeda series interprets many of the details of Morris' narration.

In 1862 Burne-Jones painted an Annunciation that elaborated on Rossetti's sexual symbolism. When considered in the symbolic scheme, his title, *The Annunciation, the Flower of God* (figure 3.6) calls attention to the flower as instrument of Holy generation and also to the deflowering of the maiden. Burne-Jones centers his composition on the flower stem as the instrument of conception. Mary kneels at her bedside; the angel Gabriel hovers on the outside of her bedroom window as he thrusts the lily stem through the window. At the picture's center the stem's end points toward Mary.

By giving the figures in Burne-Jones' *Saint George and the Dragon* (1868, figure 3.7) the same structural arrangement as *The Flower of God,* Burne-Jones links the two paintings typologically. St. George's sword substitutes for the flower of god; the dragon replaces the Virgin. The monster's writhing neck resembles Angelica's "throat let back" in Rossetti's sonnets for *Ruggiero and Angelica*; the sword penetrating its mouth has already drawn blood. The slaying is doubled in the arrow penetrating an aperture between the dragon's legs, directly under the spread legs of the Saint. In the background the princess, still tied up, appears ghostly and almost irrelevant. Another *Saint George* (1868, figure 3.8) employs the vocabulary of sacred painting. A foregrounded Princess assumes the pose of the Virgin. Her pose also echoes the triangular configuration of the dragon, suggesting that the two are counterparts. The point of a broken spear in front of the princess, similar in shape to the tail of the dragon in Rossetti's window design,

3.6. Edward Burne-Jones, *The Annunciation, the Flower of God*
Courtesy of Roy Miles.

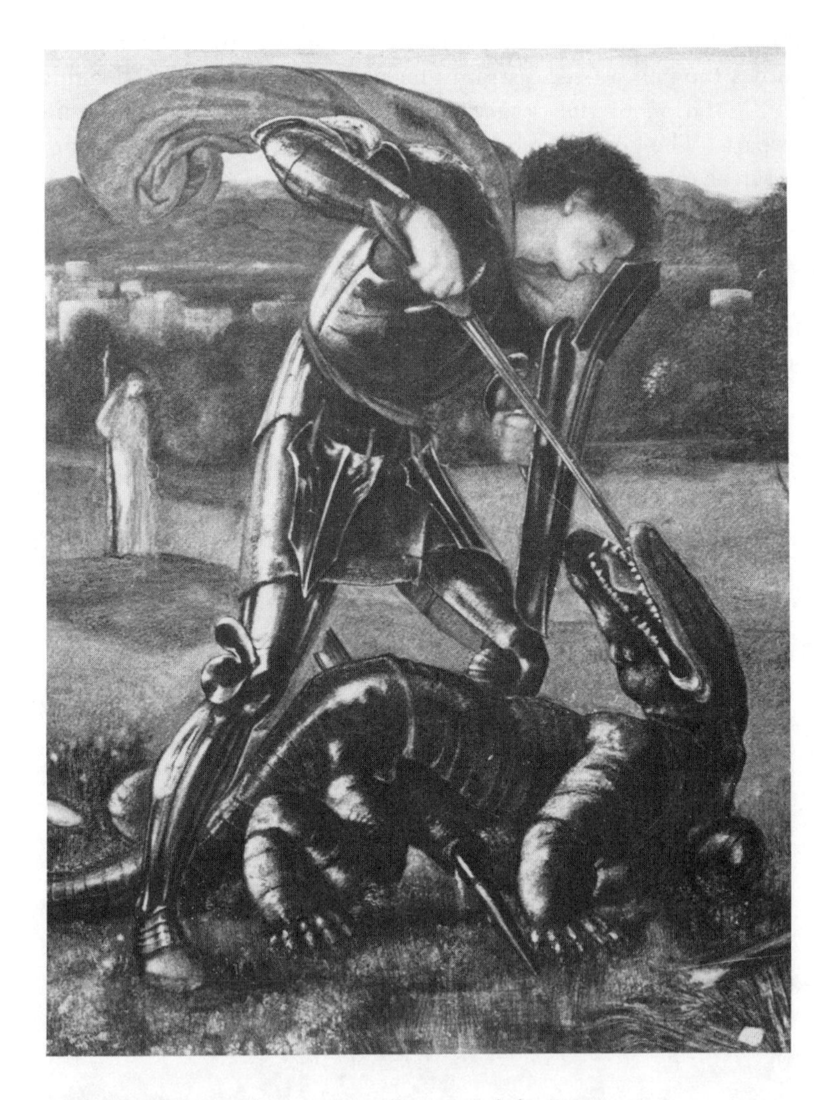

3.7. Edward Burne-Jones, *Saint George and the Dragon*
Reproduced with permission of the William Morris Gallery, Walthamstow, London.

are fragmented sexual symbols—the phallic point of the spear's "stem."

Making yet another typological connection combining classical and biblical figures, the 1876–79 *Annunciation* links Eve, Venus, and Mary (figure 3.9). Mary wears a Grecian robe: above her head on the arch is a depiction of the Expulsion from Van Eyck. Here Burne-Jones alludes to orthodox iconographic typology where Mary fulfills the promise of the fallen Eve. Mary assumes the pose of a Venus, the well beside her performing the function of the column on which antique statues of the goddess have her resting her hands. Like the descent of Perseus, Gabriel quietly comes down from the sky, a placid lowering, as if he were standing on a transparent elevator. The angle of Gabriel's head resembles the St. George, and their expressions are similarly benevolent.

3.8. Edward Burne-Jones, *Saint George*
Reproduced with permission of the British Museum.

As Rossetti had searched for romance words, in a similar fashion Burne-Jones examined the typological iconography of illuminated manuscripts where he could see the correspondence between Eve, Mary, and Andromeda. An example of this typology can be found in the Strasbourg Chronicle of 1597–1614: in a central lunette Eve gives the forbidden fruit to Adam, with the snake coiling around the tree, while in two flanking lunettes Perseus slays the serpent and Andromeda, chained, awaits her rescuer.[41] Scriptural Eve and classical Andromeda are typologically linked.[42] Burne-Jones includes elements of Genesis in his Perseus series, also alluding to classical statuary in the attitudes of Andromeda and Mary.

Burne-Jones' Andromeda in the rescue scene of his Perseus series assumes the pose of the goddess of love, the same pose as his Mary assumed as she stood by the well in his *Annunciation.* His nude Andromeda, viewed from the back, rests her arms on a part of the rock, as if it were a pedestal, similar to the well in the *Annunciation.*

Burne-Jones selects events from the Perseus story to connect the hero's quest for the Medusa to the freeing of Andromeda. While Perseus slays the dragon with a sword Medusa's head bulges in a wallet, partly discernible around his midriff. Burne-Jones emphasizes the stoniness of the myth, alluding to the female monster herself and to the stiffness she causes in men. In *The Rock of Doom* (1884–88) Perseus has just descended to observe the maiden. The tide is low and one can see a city in the background. Perseus removes his helmet to gaze at Andromeda. The rock to which she is chained and on which the hero rests his hand resembles Ingres' rock, here emphasizing its phallic shape. In the next picture of the series, *The Doom Fulfilled* (1888, figure 3.10), rocks envelop the figures in a confining space. The title alludes to the typological moment of fulfillment as well as to the word "doom" in Morris' title. This doom, however, does not refer to the fate of Acrisius, but rather first to the Rock and then to the monster. Slaying the

3.9. Edward Burne-Jones, *Annunciation*
Reproduced with permission of the National Museums and Galleries on Merseywide.

dragon fulfills the doom, the word itself carrying medieval undertones, denoting curse, prophesy, fate. Rock and monster are conflated.

Although dominated by the struggle between Perseus and his double, the sea serpent, the painting is divided between the earth/rock tones of the woman's side of the painting and the blackish-blue water tones of the male struggle. Man and monster merge.

3.10. Edward Burne-Jones. *The Doom Fulfilled*
Reproduced with permission of the Staatsgalerie Stuttgart.

Perseus rides the snake, the end of which pokes from between his legs, arcs above him, and rests above the head of the naked Andromeda. Burne-Jones magnifies Rossetti's stained-glass dragon-tail erection to gigantic proportions. The hero's black armor echoes the black scaliness of the monster's back. The opponents' heads resemble each other. The beast's open-mouthed hostility is muted in the hero's determined gaze while the helmet's swirls and whorls decoratively elaborate the monster's curls and wave-like projections. The serpent's profile mirrors Perseus' helmeted head.

In the last picture of the series, *The Baleful Head* (1888, figure 3.11) the implicit comparison between Medusa and Andromeda becomes explicit. A clothed Andromeda holds Perseus' hand whose other hand holds the Medusa's head aloft while Andromeda looks down a well at its reflection. The series of allusions make typological connections between Andromeda, Mary, and Eve. The well alludes to Mary at a similarly shaped well in the Annunciation painting, and apples fallen from the tree in the background allude to the expulsion from Eden, typologically represented in that same painting. The whole scene takes place in a garden—the typological parallel to Mary's and Eve's gardens. Perseus gazes ardently at Andromeda who wears the blue robe conventionally worn by Mary. Biblical and classical story have been assimilated to a Victorian ethos not usually associated with the Aesthetics. The scene is mannerly, even bourgeois. Muting the possibilities for terror in depicting the viewing of Medusa, Burne-Jones' representation takes its mood from the intimacy of its space, where limitation would prevent extravagant evil. Even the word "baleful" reduces the malignancy of the Gorgon's curse, since it connotes mourning as well as wickedness.

Rossetti, Morris, and Burne-Jones represent attraction as well as danger in Medusa. The violence implicit in the myth's action has been calmed, where the walled garden converts Andromeda's dangerous bondage to a rock to a safe confinement for two. In *The Baleful Head* Perseus firmly grasps the Medusa's beautiful head, gazing ardently at Andromeda's living head while she looks at the reflection of the severed head with calm pleasure. No longer uncivilized, the threat, though present, is submerged. Medusa is alluded to in the stoniness of the landscape and functions as a subtext of the theme of sexual initiation. Petrification is a theme of Burne-Jones' Perseus cycle, a sexual petrification associated with Medusa. Rossetti's search for "stunners" as he referred specifically

3.11. Edward Burne-Jones, *The Baleful Head*
Reproduced with permission of the Staatsgalerie, Stuttgart.

to certain women is summed up in the idea of Medusa, stunner of men.

"Aspecta Medusa," Rossetti's picture and poem on Perseus showing the head of Medusa to Andromeda, presents an almost anticlimactic tableau of the fate of the fatal woman, emphasizing how saving Andromeda actually rescues Perseus from the frightening aspect of her mirror image and revealing what is submerged in Burne-Jones' picture. Marriage tames, a theme of the first line of the poem: "Andromeda, by Perseus saved and wed." Read in conjunction with the title, that line makes clear that Andromeda is an aspect of Medusa.

Andromeda wards off Medusan danger in a literal way in a rarely cited painting, Burne-Jones' *Saint George* (1877, figure 3.12). The composition is influenced by the brass rubbings of which Morris was fond and which decorated the walls of their shared studio.[43] The hieratic figure of the saint occupies the entire canvas and has incorporated all the elements of the myth. Burne-Jones conflates the myths of St. George and the Dragon with Perseus and Andromeda by means of conventional typological iconography. The sinuous and naked Andromeda on the shield emphasizes the sexuality of both the princess and the maiden. Whereas Princess Sabra, freed by St. George, traditionally assumes the pose of the hapless maiden or even of the Virgin herself in prayer, Andromeda is pointedly naked, her body sensuously curved. Rather than being a scene of action, it is a painting of a symbolic internalized myth. The symbols of androgyny, representing the threat of sexuality, are now heroic attributes that are assimilated to the saint as an aegis to ward off danger.

As the Aesthetics' myth of St. George is the Andromeda myth as Pater's monk had told it, so Burne-Jones' painting merges its pagan and medieval sources. The painting is deceptively still, illustrating how the Aesthetics turned violence into decoration and merged sexual identities as a way of containing a danger. Although the naked Andromeda is probably intended to be a picture of the myth that covers most of the shield, the proportions of the maiden and the monster also make possible a reading of the shield

as a mirror, reflecting a scene at a short distance from the hero. According to that reading, St. George poses for his portrait as if he has been petrified by what he sees, as if he has gazed directly at Medusa and has suffered her curse. Dwarfing the Saint, the enormous pike, extending beyond the limit of the canvas, echoes his erect pose.

St. George's shield rests prominently in the center of the painting; its allusions further elaborate the connection between the Medusa and Andromeda. Medusa served as an aegis on the shield of Athena, warding off the dangers to the virgin goddess who identified herself with male privilege. In Burne-Jones the woman on the shield is not decapitated, but with her conventionally alluring pose, she is equally frightening as Medusa.[44] The composite image of woman and serpent serves as an emblem of woman's combined attraction and repulsion, as in Lamia, Scylla, and Medusa.[45] The snakes that coil around Medusa's head coil around Andromeda's entire body. As an aegis she wards off the evil of which she is a symbol, protecting St. George. The shield merges the image of virgin Andromeda, dragon, and Medusa. As Burne-Jones obliterates the distinction between pagan Andromeda and Christian princess, so he denies sexual difference. Not merely stiffened, St. George looks androgynous and angelic. His cape billows behind him like Gabriel's wings; his face resembles Andromeda's in *The Doom Fulfilled.*

IN THE context of fears about sexuality and its consequent projection onto female virginity, the androgynous quality of Aesthetic painting can be understood as an avoidance of sexual difference, warding off the danger of mature sexuality between equal partners. At the risk of sterility, these later Victorians retold a story of the merging of sexes by reviving the fantastic creature, the hermaphrodite. Pater described the hermaphrodite as "a kind

3.12. Edward Burne-Jones, *Saint George*
Courtesy of the Wadsworth Atheneum, Hartford. The Ella Gallup Sumner and Mary Catlin Sumner Collection.

of moral sexlessness, a kind of ineffectual wholeness of nature."[46] Swinburne defended the double nature of Dante Gabriel Rossetti as both painter and poet but compared the possible sterility of his dual gift to "that sweet marble monster of both sexes."[47] The hermaphrodite possesses its other by assimilating it to its own body. But the price is to be an anomaly, a sterile monster. It assimilates difference without obliterating its identifying signs.

In referring to Rossetti's ekphrastic poems, Oscar Wilde wittily commented on a similar duality: "to know what one really believes, one must speak through lips different from one's own."[48] The Aesthetics speak through the lips of the monster, much as the spear makes Rossetti's dragon thing speak, much as the annunciation's act speaks through lilies and flies, or as Medusa can speak through a mirror of the tame Andromeda. Aesthetic typology presents peaceful reality speaking in a decorous voice of the violence and risk of the sexual encounter.

In their retellings of the stories of the Andromeda and St. George, the Aesthetics spoke of conflicts of fleshliness in their own times through lips different from (but the same as) their own. Liberating the maiden raised questions, created ambiguities which they represented in the mergings and the blendings of their typological representations. The typological shadow provides a surface fascination to rival Medusa's allure. Rossetti's poem on the Medusa delivers a moral caution that his followers adumbrated in pictures and poems:

> Let not thine eyes know
> Any forbidden thing itself, although
> It once should save as well as kill: but be
> Its shadow upon life enough for thee

The forbidden "thing" is the Gorgon Medusa, but it is also Morris' "mass" and Burne-Jones' androgynous creatures. The Medusa's "shadow" and reflection is also the tamed Andromeda—married and sanctified passion. "Shadow," too, is another word for "figure" or "type" and suggests that the typological representation of the saving and killing woman mutes her danger. Aesthetic typology recommends substitution, representation, the mirror of art for "knowing" the forbidden thing itself. Rossetti's poem presents Aesthetic typology as defense against deflowering a virgin, thereby releasing the forbidden power of female desire.

CHAPTER FOUR

Celestial Emblems

N HIS story "The Private Life," Henry James sets the two Victorian lions, Robert Browning and Frederic Leighton, as reverse sides of an aesthetic coin. The poet and painter met in Italy where they discovered shared tastes, among others, for rescue themes. Browning's fascination with the Andromeda myth extended throughout his career; Leighton painted two canvases, one of Perseus flying to the rescue, the other of Andromeda, Perseus, and the monster. In the late 1860s the two friends attended together Gluck's *Alceste*. Afterward they both recreated the myth of a virtuous wife rescued from death. In *Balaustion's Adventures* (1871), Browning's rendering of Euripides's *Alcestis,* the poet compared the controlled strength of Leighton's *Hercules Wrestling with Death for the Body of Alcestis* (1869–70) to his own rougher version:

> strong
> As Heracles, though rosy with a robe
> Of grace that softens down the sinewy strength.[1]

Leighton's *Self-Portrait* (1880) in bright red Oxford robes comments on Browning's evaluation, the rosy robes and classical curls across his large brow suggesting a lion from the antique, authoritative yet controlled.

In James' story Browning is Clare Vawdry, a great writer but a second-rate personality, whose literary genius creates in lofty solitude at the same moment as his double stupifies social gatherings with vacuous talk. Leighton, or Lord Mellifont in the story, impeccable, glorious looking, and a public artist of the first rank, disappears when he is alone, having no subjective identity apart from a validating audience.

James conceives of the two men as extremes of a common problem. In different ways both poet and painter seem disconnected from their work. James imagined that the poet could not be the true maker of his great poems, since he was a personality not a true person:

> He used to be called "subjective" . . . , but in society no distinguished man could have been less so. He never talked about himself; and this was a topic on which, . . . he apparently never even reflected. He had his hours and his habits, . . . but all these things together never made up an attitude. . . . *He* was exempt from variations . . . He differed from other people, but never from himself . . . and struck me as having neither moods nor sensibilities nor preferences.[2]

A contemporary French art critic, Robert de La Sizeranne, characterizes Leighton's work as similarly missing a developing center, a lack making impossible the differing from previous work that creates an *oeuvre*'s depth. Leighton's self-consciously constructed home, observes the critic, is a "Temple of Eclecticism," consisting of attitudes, of various times and of various civilizations: "It is a Pantheon with altars devoted to all forms of art, to all esthetic gods, and one methodically scans the temple, searching for an empty altar, dedicated to 'the unknown God.' "[3] He also found Leighton's paintings allusive without having a powerful interpretative perspective.

Both painter and poet left an impression of there being some void in their work. Criticism of Browning has searched for his true God revealed, perhaps, in code. In their eclectic, multifaceted art they both represented other beings, other times, disowned by Robert Browning as "so many utterances of imaginary persons, not mine."[4] In part a resistance to autobiographical interpretation, Browning's disclaimer apparently cedes authority over his poetic voice. Similarly Leighton's paintings present imaginary scenes, recreate other worlds, and adapt styles of European masters. They, too, seem to speak in many voices, none of them the painter's. Like Browning's monologues, they seem absent of a coherent creating subjectivity, as if they, like Browning's work, verge on modernity.[5]

James describes the handsome painter, as beautiful as one of his paintings, as giving the age an idol to venerate: "the mere sound of his name and air of his person, the general expectation he created, were, somehow, too exalted to be verified . . . The handsomest man of his period could never have looked better . . . He pervaded [English public life], he coloured it, he embellished it, and without him it would scarcely have had a vocabulary. Certainly it would not have had a style."[6] James suggests that Leighton's is a style without the man.

What their contemporary critics perceived as lack might be usefully regarded as a gap in the two men's symbolic system, filled instead by a counter-discourse, the semiotic. Their use of emblematic objects as interpretative devices produces a discourse, employed by both artist and poet to suggest a viewpoint without intruding on the seeming objectivity of their works. Although he is sparing in their use, Leighton's emblematic objects give meaning to paintings that otherwise seem only gorgeous surface without depth. Browning adapts an emblematic method to give his work an authority distinct from the utterance of his imaginary persons.

Differing from illustrated poems or captioned pictures, emblems consist of an image or *impresa* and glossing text, sometimes summarized by a motto (figure 4.1), the whole constituting a unified work of art. Each element gives the whole a sense of inevitable truth, the aphoristic motto summarizing its wisdom. Emblem writers invoked the model of Egyptian hieroglyphics, thinking its ideographs were more immediately communicative than phonetic signs and yet were more mysterious, a coded language of a priesthood. In the seventeenth century, Francis Quarles' *Hieroglyphics of the Life of Man* links its glossed pictures to Egyptian ideographs, asserting a power of a semiotic system different from a phonetic alphabet. Emblem writers thus invoked the combined powers of written and visual language to transcend ordinary symbolic meaning. Often they referred to the emblematic image as the body and the written text as the soul of the unified work. The whole, they thought, was larger than the sum of its separate parts. Since the meaning of the symbolic image is not available to the ordinary viewer or reader, the function of the glossing text is particularly important. Lacking a written gloss, emblematic objects in paintings frequently reveal themselves by a scale different from the rest of the painting.

In both Browning and Leighton the emblematic object stands apart in their work as another kind of discourse. The emblematic object functions in a manner analogous to what Julia Kristeva defines as the semiotic. Existing in a nonlinguistic realm, the semiotic marker requires symbolic discourse to articulate its meaning in the way that an emblematic image, or *impresa,* requires the glossing text. To determine "a hieroglyphic semiotic practice" in discourse, one notices what Kristeva calls "conjunctive disjunction," a position connected to the cultural position of women:

> There would be evidence showing influence of a hieroglyphic semiotic practice based on "conjunctive disjunction" . . . Such hieroglyphic semiotic practice is also and above all a conjunctive disjunction of the two sexes as irreducibly differentiated and, at the same time, alike. This explains why, over a long period, a major semiotic practice of Western society . . . attributed to the Other (Woman) a *primary* structural role.[7]

As soone, as wee to bee, begunne;
We did beginne, to be Vndone.

ILLVSTR. XLV. *Book.* I.

WHen some, in former Ages, had a meaning
An *Emblem*, of *Mortality*, to make,
They form'd an *Infant*, on a *Deaths-head* leaning,
And, round about, encircled with a *Snake.*
The *Childe* so pictur'd, was to signifie,
That, from our very *Birth*, our *Dying* springs:
The *Snake*, her *Taile devouring*, doth implie
The *Revolution*, of all Earthly things.
For, whatsoever hath *beginning*, here,
Beginnes, immediately, to vary from
The same it was; and, doth at last appeare
What very few did thinke it should become.
The solid *Stone*, doth molder into *Earth*,
That *Earth*, e're long, to *Water*, rarifies;
That *Water*, gives an *Airy Vapour* birth,
And, thence, a *Fiery-Comet* doth arise:
That, moves, untill it selfe it so impaire,
That from a *burning-Meteor*, backe againe,
It sinketh downe, and thickens into *Aire*;
That *Aire*, becomes a *Cloud*; then, *Drops of Raine*:
Those *Drops*, descending on a *Rocky-Ground*,
There, settle into *Earth*, which more and more,
Doth harden, still; so, running out the *round*,
It growes to be the *Stone* it was before.
Thus, All things wheele about; and, each *Beginning*,
Made entrance to it owne *Destruction*, hath.
The *Life* of *Nature*, entreth in with *Sinning*;
And, is for ever, wayted on by *Death*:
The *Life* of *Grace*, is form'd by *Death* to *Sinne*;
And, there, doth *Life-eternall*, straight beginne.

Though

Kristeva's definition of the semiotic connects gender to modes of discourse. She argues that hieroglyphic construction as another order of meaning informs the cultural construction of gender, ultimately fusing Other (woman) to Same (man) by the process of male projection, while the same process excludes the Other as woman. In contrast to the distancing of allegory and the merging of differences in typology, emblematic interpretations claim to decode territory outside language, requiring male or symbolic discourse to elucidate the female or semiotic sign.

The power of emblems, I will argue, embodies for Browning the kind of power he defines as feminine. Leighton, too, uses emblematic objects to express what his eclectic vocabulary cannot directly impart. Both poet and painter employ emblematic objects to control the meaning of their seemingly objective art. The private life or subjective center James portrayed as missing can be discerned in the silent voice of emblems. That voice, as Kristeva defines it, as Browning explicates it, and as Leighton's emblematic objects reveal, occupies the position of a female Other.

Robert Browning's Constellation

NO VICTORIAN has been so identified with the Perseus and Andromeda myth as Robert Browning; to many it seemed as if the poet had constructed his life to fulfill the promise encoded in the ancient myth. Allusions to it in his poetry precede his rescue of Elizabeth Barrett Barrett from the death grip of her father. William C. DeVane traced Browning's allusions to Perseus and Andromeda throughout his poetry and connected the romance in the myth to the poets' elopement yet failed to notice that the similarity between the poets' life and the myth did not end with marriage.[8] First the chivalrous rescuer, Perseus then became devoted husband and doting father who relinquished his throne when his son came of age. Browning, too, appeared willing to abdicate his eminence for the sake of his son's career. "Do you know," the

4.1. George Wither, Emblem XLV
Courtesy of the Beinecke Rare Book and Manuscript Library, Yale University.

poet confided to a friend "if the thing were possible, I would renounce all personal ambition and would destroy every line I ever wrote, if by so doing I could see fame and honor heaped on my Robert's head."[9] Browning apparently emulated his exemplar, Perseus, to the end.

Elizabeth Barrett Browning may have been aware that Robert required a damsel to rescue. She also shared his concept of heroic rescue, imagining a rescue scene long before the real hero insisted his way into her chamber. "At five I supposed myself a heroine," the fourteen-year-old Elizabeth confided in a short autobiographical sketch, "and in my day dreams of bliss I constantly imaged to myself a forlorn damsel in distress rescued by some noble knight."[10] Elizabeth's daydream may imagine herself as both rescuing knight and forlorn damsel. Years later in the *Sonnets from the Portuguese,* which pays homage to her husband's redemptive power, the rescuer is more certainly a male. The weeping woman is rescued by Love, not Death (*Sonnets,* I) as the rescuer's miraculous "saving kiss . . . retrieves" the woman and returns her to the world she lost (*Sonnets,* XXVII). Barrett Browning suggests that she fitted herself into the role that a biographer without irony called "Andromeda in Wimpole Street."[11]

In a later sonnet Barret Browning appeals to a male heroic rescuer, this time an artist. She wrote an ekphrastic sonnet on Hiram Powers' *The Greek Slave* (1843, figure 4.2) after she had seen the original in the American sculptor's Florentine studio. Powers' statue represents the sale into prostitution of Caucasian Greek maidens by oriental Turks, a familiar subject for paintings of the period. The Greek slave averts her head without lowering it, assuming a neoclassical attitude. The statue refines away any uncouth reference to its overtly sexual subject, while its smooth marble surface erases anything but the most genteel reminders of sexual difference.

Barrett Browning's sonnet, published in 1850, only alludes to the specific subject of sexual slavery, mentioning the maiden's "enshackled hands" and "man's crimes." She uses the statue as occasion to echo the neoclassical maxim that beauty inspires man-

4.2. Hiram Powers, *The Greek Slave*
Courtesy of the Yale University Art Gallery. The Olive Louise Dann Fund.

kind to nobility, smoothing away immediate passions and specific horrors. She issues a cry to freedom by praising Art's moral power:

> Pierce to the centre,
> Art's fiery finger!—and break up ere long
> The serfdom of this world! Appeal, fair stone,
> From God's pure heights of beauty against man's wrong![12]

The sonnet gives power to the "fair stone," to the power of the artist's shaping to rescue the world from all kinds of servitude. Barrett Browning uses the female slave as a symbol of all slavery, while suggesting that the unmentioned subject of female sexual slavery is a worldwide male crime. The poet credits the artist with an ability to purify that evil by sculpting an ideal woman, almost a personification. Barrett Browning calls *The Greek Slave*'s style "passionless perfection," defining an artistry whose moral suasion, like that of Kingsley's "Triumph of Woman," has redemptive power to "strike and shame the strong,/By thunders of white silence, overthrown" (ll. 13–14). In defining the power of the statue, Barrett Browning alludes to its semiotic power, existing not on the linguistic level but in stone silence, speaking chastely in the powerful eloquence of art. Its silent power issues a rescue call reliant on the male sculptor's articulation.

Like the sculptor's moral power, Robert Browning's many allusions to the Andromeda myth have been considered as presenting paradigms for proper human behavior. In *The Ring and the Book,* for example, frequent allusions to the mythological characters, Perseus, Andromeda, and the monster, represent absolute moral positions, counterbalancing the relativism of the differing viewpoints of the poem's monologuists. That Caponsacchi is a Perseus/St. George figure tells the reader to believe in his goodness; that she is likened to Andromeda confers upon Pompilia blameless victimhood. When regarded in this way Browning's interpretation of the myth reenacts a Victorian melodrama, complementary to Barrett Browning's sonnet, complete with gender stereotypes. Politically liberal in the tradition of Shelley's redemptive vision, Browning's Perseus opposes tyranny of the strong over the weak, conforming to Victorian conventions of manliness. Browning also used the myth in less conventional, more complicated, ways.

Rather than rehearse the familiar story of saving man and saved woman by tracing rescue themes and allusions to the Andromeda myth in Browning's work, my focus will be on the emblematic interpretation of a specific Perseus and Andromeda etching which acted as a muse for Browning's poetry up to the time he actually rescued his wife. Many themes become attached to the idea of Andromeda during his career, culminating in his final invocation of the image in his last major work. Browning uses the etching from *Perseus et Andromede* by Polidoro da Caravaggio (figure 4.3) as the central image in a complex of signs he interprets as female. Making the Andromeda figure into an emblem of his poetics, he uses it as chivalric token to inspire great feats of poetry. As the sign of Browning's literary power, Andromeda is his aesthetic signature, a figure for his taking in, even taking over, female power.

An early letter to Miss Barrett illustrates how Browning incorporates the Andromeda figure into an emblematic image. Using the Andromeda etching in association with other personally meaningful objects, Browning describes the place at his parents' home where he wrote all his poetry. Out of his precious things, the poet makes an emblematic picture, the various scales of the objects contributing to a surreal portrait of his mind. He glosses the symbolic scene as emblematic of his own particular power to evoke a world of meaning mysteriously couched in personal objects:

> Who told you of my skull and spider webs—Horne? Last year I petted extraordinarily a fine fellow, (a *garden* spider—there was the singularity,—the thin clever-even-for a spider-sort, and they are *so* "spirited and sly," all of them—this kind makes a long cone of web, with a square chamber of vantage at the end, and there he sits loosely and looks about)—a great fellow that housed himself, with real gusto, in the jaws of a great skull, whence he watched me as I wrote. . . . Phrenologists look gravely at that great skull, by the way, and hope, in their grim manner, that its owner made a good end. It looks quietly, now, out at the green little hill behind. I have no little insight to the feelings of furniture, and treat books and

> prints with a reasonable consideration—how some people use their pictures, for instance is a mystery to me—very revolting all the same: portraits obliged to face each other for ever,—prints put together in portfolios . . . my Polidoro's perfect Andromeda along with "Boors Carousing," by Ostade,—where I found her,—my own father's doing, or I would say more.[13]

Browning makes an *impresa* of his writing place, glossing it to create an emblem of his poetic soul. The macabre scene contains a skull, a male (rather than a female) spider in a web, and Polidoro's perfect Andromeda. The objects require the emblem maker's explication in which he creates a composite image, associating Death, a predatory creature, Andromeda, false science, and art. Although the letter does not fully elucidate the meaning of his symbolic picture, Browning suggests that the power of art, personified by Andromeda, rescues the writer from the threat posed by the skull and the spider, suggestions confirmed by emblematic interpretations in two works appearing fifty-four years apart, in 1833 and in 1887.

4.3. Etching after Polidoro da Caravaggio, *Perseus et Andromede*

A dream recounted in *Pauline* demonstrates how Browning connects gender identity to artistic power. The passage prepares for an emblem with Andromeda as central figure later in the poem. The speaker in *Pauline* confesses to dreaming of himself as a beautiful naked woman whom he calls a witch. Browning distances the dangers to his masculinity of imagining himself as a woman, first by reporting the story as the dream of a troubled speaker, and second by emphatically and repeatedly insisting that the speaker is not the poet.

The male speaker resembles a young poet like Browning in that he too is a Romantic quester with an evangelical conscience. He dreams that he is a beautiful female witch who draws down from the sky a male god and then ferociously diminishes him:

> I was a young witch, whose blue eyes,
> As she stood naked by the river springs,
> Drew down a god—I watched his radiant form
> Growing less radiant—and it gladdened me;
> Till one morn, as he sat in the sunshine
> Upon my knees, singing to me of heaven,
> He turned to look at me, ere I could lose
> The grin with which I viewed his perishing.
> And he shrieked and departed, and sat long
> By his deserted throne—but sunk at last,
> Murmuring, as I kissed his lips and curled
> Around him, "I am still a god—to thee."
> (ll. 112–23)

Like Andromeda, the witch stands naked at the margin of earth and water, attracting a god-like man from the heavens as irresistibly as if she were a magnetic force. But there the similarity to the myth seems to end. Rather than the heavenly descender rescuing the naked young witch, she destroys him while he retains his power over her: "I am still a god—to thee."

The witch's spell turns the god into a dependent child sitting on her knees. Evoking primitive infantile emotions, the scene exemplifies Melanie Klein's concept of envy, involving not simply the desire to possess what the other has but the desire to harm the envied other. At the end of the passage the pronouns are sufficiently ambiguous that the "I" of the last line could almost refer to the witch. Confusingly and primitively merged, the witch curls around the god.

Admitting that the "I" is himself: "I was a young witch," the male dreamer gives a female gender to his own envious desire. While defining his desire as compelling, he sees it also as a destructive Other. Blissfully unaware of her envy, the god sacrifices his radiance to her. The dream confesses to vicious emotions, projected from the male self onto a female witch. Hannah Segal describes the emotion that incorporates the object as "envy fused with greed, making for a wish to exhaust the object entirely, not only in order to possess all its goodness but also to deplete the object purposefully so that it no longer contains anything enviable."[14] At the end of the dream, envy fails to overwhelm the dreamer's adoration; in more than one sense, the god has the last word. Diminished or not, he retains his divinity, even as the "I" curls around him, taking him in.[15]

The speaker bears the marks of guilt attendant upon his ferocious desires to incorporate the god and to deplete him. Like the poem in general, the dream is about the power of poetry, shown in the dream to be appropriative. The guilty dreamer confesses—the subtitle is *Fragment of a Confession*—to the murderous emotions he believes are required to make himself into a poet. By the end of the poem the speaker has discovered his life goal, "to be a lover and a poet, as of old," in the course of the poem confessing in various ways to the dangers of the poetic enterprise. To capture the radiant song of the god, the speaker believes that he needs a power identified with femininity, but that identification denotes a cultural diminishment. Aspiring to fame, the male poet gives up his culturally dominant masculine position to identify with the second sex.

Insofar as *Pauline* concerns Browning's exhilarating discovery and involvement with Shelley's poetry, the dream expresses the younger poet's attraction to the etherealized singer, who appeared as a "radiant god" to be emulated. The highly charged emotionality of the passage and its mythopoeic eroticism is Shelleyan.[16] Like a young god, Shelley sang to Browning who imitated Shelley's atheism and vegetarianism until, like the naked witch, he was forced to drive Shelley from his throne. Although Browning rejected his Shelleyan pose, the "Sun-Treader" was still a god to the younger poet, who fought to replace this "radiant form" with his Protestant God.[17] The witch both worships and destroys this Percy/Perseus.

Pauline's dream presents a paradigm of poetic appropriation, imagined in terms of taking over female power. This same paradigm is exemplified in the interpretative process whereby the poet constructs an emblem from the Perseus and Andromeda etching. The figure of Andromeda becomes an emblem of an expressive power associated with the feminine. Rather than make the characters in the Andromeda myth into dramatic figures, the poet uses them as emblematic ciphers, susceptible to the poet's interpretation. By interpreting the characters as if they were figures of an *impresa* Browning turns the image of Polidoro's Andromeda into a sign of male creativity. By using Andromeda's attributes—her chains, her nakedness, her hair—as emblematic objects, the poet gestures to elements in the myth and interprets their meaning as if he were an emblem writer. As an emblematic device, Andromeda becomes a sign of his poetic genius.

In *Pauline* the Andromeda picture becomes the *impresa* for an emblematic illustration of the plight of a young artist. Seeking a vocation, *Pauline*'s guilt-ridden speaker finds that looking at Polidoro's Andromeda gives him proof of a stability which steadies his own faltering identity. He discovers evidence of permanence in Polidoro's monumental Andromeda. At first emblematic of the poet's concern with poetic origins, Andromeda appears at that point in *Pauline* when the speaker, who desires a place in the company of great artists, has canvassed all arts, only to feel alienated, aging, and incapable of freeing himself from aspirations to be a god among poets.

The speaker ultimately chooses the goal of lover (later changed to poet) and prophet, but he has clearly wanted more of everything the world offers. Like many other of Browning's *personae,* this speaker confesses to insatiable desire, gnawing, infinite, and associated with hunger: "my hunger for/All pleasure, howsoe'er minute" (ll. 602–3). Awareness of mortality "chains" his desires. The speaker decides to moderate boundless desire, to focus upon "one rapture." His "still-decaying frame" forces him to be one person when he would be many, to concentrate upon one art when he would practice them all. He knows that such unity not only compromises his desires but lies about reality, limits full vision, and denies full pleasure. Withering into an acceptance of mortality, he settles for "Some pleasure, while my soul could grasp the world,/But must remain this vile form's slave" (ll. 616–17).

The poet's association to Andromeda emerges from the conflict of what he feels as his soul's capacity against his body's limitations. His restless passion lies within him, "a chained thing." Rather than conceiving himself as a slave to his passions, he imagines his passions as "my bright slave," hemmed in by the mortal coil.[18] His own too human condition resembles the picture of the chained maiden's plight. She represents his passion chained by the bondage of decaying flesh. Not only bound by the chains of mortality, flesh is also constrained by the monster, called in this poem a "snake," suggestive in this guilty poem of Miltonic Sin. Browning refers to the sea monster as "the snake" as he turns to Polidoro's etching:

> Andromeda!
> And she is with me: years roll, I shall change,
> But change can touch her not—so beautiful
> With her fixed eyes, earnest and still, and hair
> Lifted and spread by the salt-sweeping breeze,
> And one red beam, all the storm leaves in heaven
> Resting upon her eyes and hair, such hair,
> As she awaits the snake on the wet beach
> By the dark rock and the white wave just breaking
> At her feet; quite naked and alone; a thing
> I doubt not, nor fear for, secure some god
> To save will come in thunder from the stars.
> (ll. 656–67)

Browning describes Andromeda as monumental, earnest, and still, not as Kingsley's shivering girl nor as Hopkins' tortured one, but as a woman, solitary and proud. Indeed, Polidoro's Andromeda, who does not look helpless, dominates the picture plane. Starkly in the center of the composition, her hefty legs planted on the rock, her chin defiantly aloft, she neither importunes her descending deliverer nor gazes at her intended devourer. Meager in comparison to the damsel in distress, Perseus hovers in the air. The heoric slaying occurs in a corner; Perseus' cutlass descends airily upon the monster, a largish worm who seems almost to anticipate the slaying by curling up. The tenacious roots at the left, the ripples of waves curling around the rock, and the coiling dragon echo the hair motif, emphasizing the electric waves of Andromeda's flowing hair.

By ignoring the temporal sequence in the etching—Andromeda's parents in the left and Perseus who drops down from the sky like "some god"—Browning emphasizes Andromeda's solitude. He focuses on two of her attributes: hair (mentioned three times) and nakedness. Hair for Browning is a figure of mortality. The musing speaker in "A Toccata of Galuppi's," for example, uses the phrase "such hair" to remind himself of the poignancy of the decaying body's sexuality:

> "Dust and ashes!" So you creak it, and I want the heart to scold.
> Dear dead women, with such hair, too—what's become of all the gold
> Used to lie and brush their bosoms? I feel chilly and grown old.
>
> (ll. 43–45)

For the aging speaker hair signifies the gold of vital female sexuality. As in *Pauline,* his sigh, "such hair," evokes the skull looming behind such hair—dust and ashes.

Gold in conjunction with hair is directly associated with death in "Gold Hair: A Story of Pornic," where a dead woman's golden hair is a sign of her earthly vanity and greed, a counterpart of the golden coins which the dying maiden hid in her magnificent tresses as a refusal to acknowledge mortality:

> X
>
> And lo, when they came to the coffin-lid,
> Or rotten planks which composed it once,
> Why, there lay the girl's skull wedged amid

A mint of money, it served for the nonce
To hold in its hair-heaps hid!

XI

Hid there? Why? Could the girl be wont
(She the stainless soul) to treasure up
Money, earth's trash and heaven's affront?
Had a spider found out the communion-cup,
Was a toad in the christening-font?

(ll. 96–105)

As in Browning's letter to Elizabeth, skull and spider are emblematic objects. The skull peers atop the virgin's skeleton, surrounded by the unspent coins that eventually replaced her hair. The spider evilly lurks in the communion cup.

The historically true story of Pornic reveals the skull beneath the hair, whereas *Pauline*'s Andromeda portrays such hair as still moving in the eternity of art. Polidoro's Andromeda becomes an emblem of the artist's mission to create permanence from flux. To dedicate himself as an artist enables him to transcend the flesh, to "fling age, sorrow, sickness off,/And rise triumphant, triumph through decay" (ll. 674–75).

In its paradoxical formulation "Triumph through decay" resembles many emblem mottos, such as "Make haste slowly." The motto does not seem to refer to the Andromeda myth, but since Browning's emblem alludes to a specific work of art, the motto affirms the paradox of a mortal poet overcoming death through his art. Browning opposes the Andromeda emblem to the danger represented by the spider in the communion cup and the decayed Pornic maiden's body: "change can touch her not."

As a symbol of eternity Andromeda defends aesthetic interpretation against the challenge of scientific interpretation. The meaning of Andromeda as a representation of art's "recompense" for the artist's "still decaying frame" depends upon believing in a transcendent meaning of images, a meaning that challenges scientific discourse. Like Keats' urn, Browning's Andromeda contrasts eternal art to rotting flesh. The Andromeda figure, not the Perseus figure, rescues the poet from despair. The speaker gains hope and artistic purpose by his identification with Polidoro's perfect Andromeda. As an emblem Andromeda teaches Browning a lesson of feminine power, the reward for which, he believes, is the immortality of art.

Sign and Signature

AT THE beginning of Browning's career, Andromeda represents the timelessness of art. Toward the end of his life, in the *Parleyings with Certain People of Importance in Their Day* (1887), she represents a greater permanence but a greater abstraction than Art; she represents the imagination that makes art possible. Not recognizably autobiographical, *Parleyings* includes no facts about the poet's life. Perhaps, like Wordsworth's *The Prelude,* Browning meant to chart his poetic development, but unlike Wordsworth, Browning includes no scenes of youth, no faltering steps to manhood. The poet instead struggles with ideas divorced from incidents, conjuring seven silent figures from the dead who overhear the poet tell them what he thinks of their work. The title alludes to the mutability of fame, for the invoked shades of seven historical personages who had been important to the poet's intellectual development had become obscure. The poet's understanding at the end of his life further distances these figures from him; important in the past, their relevance has faded.

The etching of Polidoro's Andromeda returns in the longest and most complex of *Parleyings,* "With Francis Furini," a work differing from the other parleyings in that the Tuscan painter did not influence the poet's early intellectual development and, unlike the other six people, the artist wrote nothing. Most of what Browning knew of the painter's life came from the writings of the art critic Filippo Balducinni who compiled a dictionary of the lives of Italian painters (1681–1728).[10] Balducinni clearly disapproved both of Furini's works and his character. A priest in his later years, Furini painted delicate and sensuous nudes—an *Andromeda* among them.

In "With Francis Furini" the Andromeda emblem appears in the context of seemingly irreconcilable themes. Defending his son against charges of painting nudes, opposing the epistemology of evolutionists, and attacking obtuse critics, Browning uses the emblem writer's gesture to evoke the Andromeda sign as a nondiscursive proof of his ability to convey the deepest truths. The Andromeda emblem attempts to unite irreconcilable but concurrent and mutually dependent ways of looking at the world.

"Parleying with Francis Furini" addresses a question of artistic propriety, specifically focused on nude painting. Should an artist paint naked women? If he does, what does the woman represent? It depends upon vision, Browning answers, and not optics. Both emblem-maker and scientist observe similar objects with a view to another meaning, a pattern outside the thing observed, but the emblematist finds a more exalted one. Evolutionists trace the exquisite female form back to simian origins. The emblematic artist observes a representation of an exquisite female form and ultimately finds God. That at least is Browning's uneasy claim.

What kind of seeing, he asks, is more profound, the view of a scientist such as an evolutionist, or the view of an artist such as the emblematist? In his search for an answer to his question, the poet explores Victorian concerns about art, science, and religion. Browning presents his final argument for an artist who trusted "signs and omens" (*Pauline,* ll. 301–2) contrasting that seer, who interprets voiceless signs, with an evolutionist who can only discern meaningless patterns, signatures without an author.

"With Francis Furini" expands upon Browning's concerns of 1835 when he constructed an imaginary biography for the philosopher/scientist Paracelsus (1493–1541), who could be considered a model for the Victorian scientist. By knowing the earth in its minute particulars, Paracelsus hoped to reach transcendent knowledge. The scientist traveled the world seeking traces and shadows of a unified truth, decipherable from the natural code written in the physical world. Browning's attraction to Paracelsus may have been based in part on the latter's theory of signatures, a theory of representation in which an object's appearance leads one to grasp its meaning. Every natural object is a signature, cipher, or character. If one understands the sign correctly and interprets it, one reveals the basic inner truth of the object.[20] Paracelsus' signatures structure the world as writing. Only a person who is chosen to decipher the code, to read the handwriting of objects, can gain a knowledge of transcendence. The world requires an emblem writer to read the meaning of the signature and to convey that essential meaning to his audience.

Paracelsus fails in his goal to decipher the signatures of the world. But he foresees the fulfillment of his goal in a future man who will be more perfect, more evolved. Browning considered that concept of human progress his version of evolution. In contrast, Darwinian evolution conflicts with a view of the textuality of nature.[21] Unlike Darwin's concept, Browning's notion of evolution is purposive, progressive, and hierarchical, more congruent with Lamarck than with Darwin.[22] Paracelsus describes Browning's Neoplatonic evolution:

> When all mankind alike is perfected,
> Equal in full-blown powers—then, not till then,
> I say, begins man's general infancy . . .
> Then shall his long triumphant march begin,
> Thence shall his being date,—thus wholly roused,
> What he achieves shall be set down to him.
> (v, ll. 741–68)

Darwinian evolution conflicts with a Paracelsan view of nature as signatures. The purpose and meaning of the universe could dissolve if the signature did not signify anything beyond itself. Without signs that add up to something, there could be no plot to human existence. Paracelsus asserts the primacy of types to oppose a nihilistic threat:

> Prognostics told
> Man's near approach; so in man's self arise
> August anticipations, symbols, types
> Of a dim splendour ever on before
> In that eternal circle life pursues.
> (v. ll. 773–77)

Without the eternal circle, history tells no story, continuing without a pattern in an infinite evolutionary straight line. Types would be utterly self-referential as isolated and particular examples of multiplicity.

In trying to reject the evolutionist view, Browning seeks a language that will encompass the minute, the bizarre, the anomaly, uniting multitudinousness in a system of signs. Perhaps the world contains an infinite vocabulary, but it constitutes a language. To reconcile evolution with eternity is a Browning project continuing throughout his career, elucidated in his second, and final, Andromeda emblem.

As a step toward that reconciliation "Cleon" (1855) addresses the themes of evolution, extinction, and transcendence, polarizing them as a debate between aesthetic and scientific interpretation. A Greek polymath of the first century, Cleon's varied and successful endeavors promise to survive his death but leave him nonetheless with insatiable hunger to live forever. He believes in evolutionary progress on earth. His art improves upon earlier art; "one lyric woman," a slave, "refines upon the women of my youth"; the cultivated "suave plum" is better than the "savage-tasted drupe." He neither finds a pattern in the earth's evolutionary progress nor can he condescend to accept the barbarian Paul's Christian promise of immortality. The skull and the spider lurk at the corners of the poem, except a human reduces to less than bones and gold coins here; he is dust shut in an urn.

Without a signature that signifies, there is no meaning to evolutionary progress. Given evidence for evolution, for human improvement over the beast, why did the gods make consciousness concomitant with unfulfillable desire?

> Malice it is not. Is it carelessness?
> Still, no. If care—where is the sign?
> (ll. 267–68)

Like Paracelsus, Cleon cannot read the signatures of nature, but he seeks a sign that the world has meaning.

In "With Francis Furini" Browning presents the sign Cleon missed by using Andromeda as a Paracelsan signature. Against those with an analytical epistemology, represented in the poem by art critics and evolutionary scientists, he presents an emblematic reading of a representation of Andromeda. Critics resemble evolutionists, since both fail to grasp the transcendent meaning of the objects they scrutinize. Emblematic vision, on the other hand, both describes the object and finds its meaning. Whereas critic and scientist, literal-minded and ignorant of true signs, can only understand the material body, the emblem maker sees soul in the body. As a poet who can translate an object's silent meaning into language, Browning invokes the figure of Andromeda chained to a rock to challenge a world full of things but emptied of significance.

Developing the motto "triumph through decay" from *Pauline,* Browning defends the "Triumph of flesh" (l. 96) against critics who do not understand the transcendent meaning of nakedness. For emblem writers nakedness could signify a spiritual attribute. The depiction of naked women, the poet argues, is an artist's tribute to the supreme aesthetic power of the Creator. Furini's paintings, so regarded, are not scientific renderings but are a form of worship:

> pictures rife
> With record, in each rendered loveliness,
> That one appreciative creature's debt
> Of thanks to the Creator more or less,
> Was paid according as heart's-will had met
> Hand's-power in Art's endeavor to express
> Heaven's most consummate of achievements, bless
> Earth by a semblance of the seal God set
> On woman his supremest work.
>
> (ll. 126–34)

"Heaven's most consummate of achievements" refers both to the creation of woman by God and to the artist's imitation of her, an imitation that identifies the artist and God by female mediation.

Nude paintings imitate unfallen nature by honoring the Creator of naked Eve. Invoking the figure of Andromeda chained to the rock, as he had in *Pauline,* Browning argues about the permanence of art. His earlier argument, however, is now inadequate. It was too concrete, dependent on an etching on a piece of paper. Instead of Furini's or Polidoro's conception of Andromeda, he points to the firmament and to the Andromeda constellation.

God traced Andromeda with stars. Comparing an artist's delineation of the maiden to the Almighty's imitation of his supremest work in the heavens, Browning claims that representations are like the celestial Andromeda. They are ideas of woman, and the artist who saw that idea in the sky received authority from God. The truest artist imposes a pattern on otherwise arbitrary signs. Interpretation of those signs is the highest form of criticism.

Only certain imaginations can discern the heavenly Andromeda. To the uninitiated eye, the night sky looks like an unconnected mass of lights. Browning compares God's creation of woman with an artist's nude paintings. Then, as if in confirmation of the sacred nature of that kind of art, he invokes the Andromeda constellation:

> soul and body's power you spent—
> Agonized to adumbrate, trace in dust
> That marvel which we dream the firmament
> Copies in star-device when fancies stray
> Outlining orb by orb, Andromeda—
> God's best of beauteous and magnificent
> Revealed to earth—the naked female form.
> (ll. 137–43)

Like emblematic images, constellations comprise a language of signs requiring a decoder with divine inspiration. To know that an assemblage of lights visible to an ordinary eye means "Andromeda" requires special knowledge, leading to truth beyond flesh. Andromeda serves Browning's purpose not only because she is a figure in a myth but also because she is a constellation. As if he were a child playing a cosmic dot-to-dot game, the artist agonizes to "trace in dust" a figure of a woman. How does he know he has made the right connections? To make interpretation not merely "fancy" but "truth" Browning requires that the imagination receive external validation.

Evolutionists offer some sort of proof, but they look in the wrong place for their evidence. They "rack nature" and emerge with a tortured, reduced answer. Lofty scientists view the lowest forms of life—atoms, protoplasm (l. 270)—and argue from that to man. Since they emphasize descent, they close off the possibility of ascent: "Have you done/Descending?" (ll. 277–78) Browning's query echoes Darwin, but his demeaning tone indicates that the poet's perspective from the vastness of cosmic spaces exposes as paltry the evolutionist's painstaking survey of physical minutiae. *Homo sapiens* appears as the supreme creation on earth, but he could be dashed from the pinnacle in an instant:

> He's at the height this moment—to be hurled
> Next moment to the bottom by rebound
> Of his own peal of laughter. All around
> Ignorance wraps him,—whence and how and why
> Things are,—yet cloud breaks and lets blink the sky
> Just overhead, not elsewhere! What assures
> His optics that the very blue which lures
> Comes not of black outside it, doubly dense?
>
> (ll. 337–44)

Browning's skepticism doubts sense perception as he posits a black hole behind the blue sky. Like Shelley's Mont Blanc and Wordsworth's spots of time, the Andromeda constellation presents to mortals the possibility of some sort of transcendent knowledge. Echoing yet changing Wordsworth's idea of tranquillity, Shelley asserts, "Power dwells apart in its tranquillity." Then he adds what is important to Browning's Andromeda: "Remote, serene, and inaccessible." Browning's Andromeda is as much the space's blankness as the more reassuring stars. Andromeda's power, too, is remote and serene, but Browning's assertion of his faith in interpretation attempts to bring that power to earth. Closed to the critical, scientific, evolutionary mind, emblematic interpretation is mysterious, needing an artist not a scientist to discern; needing intuition and not microscopic observation to understand. Andromeda, an emblem of unrepresentable black nothingness, signifies for Browning a female power unavailable to rational critics or scientists. Appropriating that power, the artist acts as a hierophant, conveying privileged information about heaven's hieroglyphics.

Browning's final vision of Andromeda refines representation to an almost pure semiotic sign. The celestial Andromeda is the opposite of Rossetti's Blessed Damozel whose breast warms the bar of heaven. She is colder than Keats' urn, the Cold Pastoral. Like Shelley's frozen Mont Blanc, she represents a terrifying blankness as well as a reassuring stability. Browning claims his own art plucks the veil of flesh to see the soul beneath. Yet, even the poet cannot be quite sure that what he showed was a permanent and not an evanescent truth:

> There did I plant my first foot. And the next?
> Nowhere! 'Twas put forth and withdrawn, perplexed
> At what seemed stable and proved stuff
> Such as the coloured clouds are:
>
> (ll. 402–5)

Like a phrenologist, the artist tries to interpret what is not visible by looking at what is. But the poet's emblematic vision may be no truer than any necromancer's claim. Browning reassures himself by returning to the image of Andromeda, but now he imagines that he is a woman in a picture who stands on a rock, wearing chains. Seeking some proof of his vision, he identifies his essential knowing self with a representation of Andromeda:

> Who proffers help of hand
> To weak Andromeda exposed on strand
> At mercy of the monster?
>
> (ll. 489–91)

The Evolutionist is the "sea-beast," and poor Browning/Andromeda clings to the rock, needing a miracle to be rescued:

> Just here my solid standing-place amid
> The wash and welter, whence all doubts are bid
> Back to the ledge they break against in foam,
>
> (ll. 509–11)

To be rescued from speaking empty signs, words without truth, a signature signifying nothing, he needs to be able to prove the pirority of symbolic reality over scientific fact. Browning turns the monster into an emblem of dangerous objective rationalism, such as evolutionists employ.

Evolutionists poke at nature to glean some minute fact as a sign of its ultimate meaning, but all they find is imitation. They scrutinize insects, for example, examining a moth with a star-pattern on its wings: "that on some insects' wing/Helps to make out in dyes the mimic star" (ll. 295–96). Looking downward from a height, evolutionists mistake the sign of a star on a bug for a signature. The emblematic imagination discovers symbolic reality, the real star, by looking from the frailty of its human condition up to the heavens:

> Look upward: this Andromeda of mine—
> Gaze on the beauty, Art hangs out for sign
> There's finer entertainment underneath.
> (ll. 529–31)

The emblem maker turns the constellation, a sign of beauty, into a signature. "Andromeda of mine" in contrast to "utterances, not mine" is a powerful erotic enticement to consider a more essential female sign, discovered by the true visionary by looking at the sea-beast. It is that ability to transform evil into a sign of transcendent good that proves the emblem maker's power over the evolutionist's:

> But what if, all at once, you come upon
> A startling proof—not that the Master gone
> Was present lately—but that something—whence
> Light comes—has pushed Him into residence?
> Was such the symbol's meaning,—old, uncouth—
> That circle of the serpent, tail in mouth?
> Only by looking low, ere looking high,
> Comes penetration of the mystery.
> (ll. 540–47)

With the gesture of a necromancer, Browning the emblematist turns the serpent, earlier in the poem an emblem of false science, into the mystical sign of ouroburos, symbol of eternity. By invoking the ancient hieroglyph of a pre-Christian belief, Browning appeals to a proof beyond rationality old, unlettered but a valid signature. The sign of Andromeda beckons us to consider an older sign, an ancient symbol of womanhood, the circle in the form of a serpent (figure 4.1).[23]

Circles are female symbols, as Browning makes explicit in "Pan and Luna." The naked Luna, illuminated by an aura, escapes from Pan's pursuit into what she thinks is a cloud; as she flees, Browning describes her body as composed of circles:

> Orbed—so the woman-figure poets call
> Because of rounds on rounds—that apple-shaped
> Head which its hair binds close into a ball
> Each side the curving ears—that pure undraped
> Pout of the sister paps—that . . . Once for all,
> Say—her consummate circle . . .
>
> (ll. 41–46)

All circles are emblematic of that consummate circle which, according to the poet's mythmaking, is not an emblem or an imitation, but is the original place of creativity. As woman is the consummate achievement of the Creator (l. 132), so the sign of human creativity is the circle, symbol of female sexuality.

The ouroboros represents the magic female power of Browning's visionary ability. He has taken an evolutionary line and has turned it into an eternal circle. His ability to change a monster into a dual symbol of woman and eternity proves his knowledge superior to the scientists. Browning "penetrates" the old, uncouth, and mysterious female sign, and claims it as a sign of his own power.

By discovering the feminine in himself, Browning returns to the quest he initiated in *Paracelsus*. He finds a symbol for that "eternal circle life pursues"—not an aimless evolution that keeps on and on endlessly through time, without rhyme or reason. By means of the semiotic, he resolves for himself an epistemological riddle he posed in 1835. Knowledge in *Paracelsus* was imagined as coming not from the world outside but from the inner self. The repetition of "in" emphasizes his point:

> There is an inmost center in us all,
> Where truth abides in fullness; and around
> Wall upon wall, the *gross flesh* hems it in,
> This perfect, clear perception—which is truth.
> A baffling and perverting carnal *mesh*
> Binds it.
>
> (Pt. I, ll. 728–33; my emphasis)

As in "With Francis Furini" imagery of clouds and mist represents the poet's difficulty in penetrating the mystery. But in the later poem the poet has resolved for himself the vexing dichotomy between what he calls "the dear fleshly perfection of the human shape" and the inner truth. The skull may be a reminder of the vanity of human wishes but the heavenly orb, like the circle, enables the poet to see beyond the baffling and perverting carnal mesh:

> the head of the adept
> May too much prize the hand, work unassailed
> By scruple of the better sense that finds
> An orb within each halo, bids *gross flesh*
> Free the fine spirit-pattern, nor *enmesh*
> More than is meet a marvel custom blends
> Only the vulgar eye to.
> (ll. 201–7; my emphasis)

By placing the crucial words of his earlier poem as end-rhymes, Browning creates closure. A nondiscursive proof, embedded in the signs and position of sounds, the rhymes create a truth beyond what the words say, appealing to magic, to a wisdom old and coarse, to spells, to charms, to chiming. As Andromeda's body deconstructs in a star sign, his defense of the signature transcends rational meaning of language.

Although the Andromeda and Perseus myth seems clearly to ascribe activity according to gender, Browning collapses the polarities: the monster turns into ourobouros, language turns into witch's chant, poet turns into naked woman. By dismantling oppositions, he appeals to the nonheroic, the nonrational, the passive, the silent. His poetics appropriates the uncouth power of the ourobouros, figured however as rescue, suggesting that the taking over improves, civilizes, articulates what had been inchoate, inexpressible, and indecipherable. But Browning also questions polarities—serpent and ourobouros, rescuer and victim, man and woman. In awe of the irrational sign that is the circle, symbol of the Other, he claims it as his own. The ourobouros and the chained maiden, like the orb (symbol of his wife in "My Star"), appeal to what Kristeva and other French feminists describe as the force of the feminine, the yet unverbalized, beyond or beneath language, at the level of the unconscious.[24] The potent silent sign is Browning's female signature.

Leighton's Sun God

FREDERIC LEIGHTON'S classical paintings reflect the artist's wholehearted veneration for the Greece of the Golden Age, as much his emulation of selected Greek values as an evocation of the past. The paintings are in part elaborated genealogical tables, illustrating a genetic tie between the race of Periclean Athens and Leightonian London. In his Royal Academy addresses, given every two years from 1879 to 1893, the president defined his theory of art, ultimately concluding that classical Greece produced the noble and the beautiful as genetic characteristics. His lectures discoursed on wide-ranging subjects, beginning with such broad inquiries as "The Position of Art in the World (1879); "Relation of Art to Morals and Religion (1881), and ending with specific evaluations of European art in Italy, Spain, France, and Germany. By the time of his third address (1883) he had prepared the way for his theory of the relationship of great art to racial traits. That lecture, "Relation of Art to Time, Place, and Racial Circumstance: Egypt, Chaldea and Greece," not only connects the quality of the art produced by a country to its genetic stock but also reveals Leighton constructing for himself his own artistic (and, by implication, genetic) pedigree.

In describing the Greeks, the eminent Victorian painter also suggests the personal significance of his classical paintings. For Leighton classical revival meant returning to origins, but not, as in Pater, an inverted homesickness, but as a return to genetic purity. As I will argue, his two paintings of the Perseus and Andromeda myth reveal a dark side of his notions of engendering, leading to a terrifying sexual meeting. By deploying embelmatic objects symbolic of generation, Leighton paints a violent and contorted myth of origin, a disturbing obverse side of the radiant coin that was his Greece.

In his lecture on the racial component of art, Leighton characterizes the static aesthetic of Egypt and Mesopotamia as "marked by a strange inertness, . . . a sluggish stream," without potency. In contrast, Greek art burst upon the world's consciousness in a fecundating eruption: "as the sudden upleaping of a living source, reflecting and scattering abroad the light of a new and a more joyous day; a spring at which men shall drink to the end of all days and not be sated."[25]

In 1879, the same year as he began the course of lectures, Leighton wrote of his change from "Gothicism to Classicism (for want of better words), i.e., a growth from multiplicity to simplicity."[26] It is no coincidence that his ascendancy to the lectern as president of the Royal Academy and his attention to a classical aesthetic occurred at the same time. Leighton thought of his change of style in the organic metaphor of growth, but his classicizing represents a change of attitude, an identification with an ideal, more than an important change of painting style. Drawing his eclectic style not so much from classical sources as from the many European capitals of art where he studied and painted, Leighton turns back to the ancients for his pedigree. He is aware of the difference between what he thinks of as a simpler Hellenistic mind and the complexities of his own evolved thought. In depicting classical subjects, however, he claims an inheritance in the upleaping life source of Greek art.

In *Venus Disrobing* (1867, figure 4.4) Leighton suggests a genetic connection between Victorian classical painting and English art. The goddess appears as a local kind of beauty, having a domesticated quality characteristic of Victorian history painting.[27] Venus does not strike quite a classical pose; the hip protrudes to the left at too exaggerated an angle; the hand touches the thigh but also coyly covers the pubic area in a manner more Victorian than Greek. Moreover, the gesture calls attention to the woman's nakedness and to the area she covers.[28] The goddess' shame gave the painting a respectability withheld from Etty's nudes, making a direct and literal connection between ancient Greece and Victorian Britain that may appear unsubtle but is not accidental. *Venus Disrobing,* as Leighton's classical paintings of women in general, can be considered as illustrations of his racial theory. The painter's notion of racial superiority resembles other Aryan theories of the times but is distinguished from them by a scientifically untenable connection between genes and gender.

Greece's miraculous gift for beauty derives from what Leighton calls the "Chemistry of Nature," meaning genetic composition, improved by careful husbandry. Aryan stock purified Greek art. The Pelasgic was "the earliest wave poured by the Aryan tide from Asia into Europe . . . followed on the scene by a purer Aryan race,"[29] the Ionians, and then another branch of the same race, the Dorians. Perfect Aryan form is balanced, having purged, as the obese Etruscans did not, any vestige of Pelasgic type.

Leighton's genetics traces Aryan blood to England and to the audience of Royal Academy students who sat before him in London. Not only were the English modern Aryans but certain English women, apparently not English men, preserve the same Aryan purity that produced the glories of Greek art: "a new ideal of balanced form wholly Aryan and of which the only parallel I know is sometimes found in the women of another Aryan race—your own."[30] Unlike Charles Kingsley who praised the "Teutons" for their blond manly vigor, Leighton conceptualizes the best qualities of his contemporary English Aryans as primarily feminine.

Venus resembles English women because of the genetic link. His Victorian Hellenes exemplify his racial and gender theory. To the idealization of women as pure moral beings—as in Ruskin's "Of Queen's Gardens" and Kingsley's "Triumph of Woman"—Leighton adds a racial component. Although he might not be able to explain his reasoning, he suggests that women transmit superior racial traits only to women. Turning English Victorian women into Greek goddesses and nymphs confirms the painter's Aryan theory. The viewer need only look at a painting to know his link with his origins in Greek vitality.

Leighton's locating Aryan purity in the English female explains in part an idealized statuesque feminine image in many of his paintings. Even if a painting is not specifically classical in theme, the depiction itself of that Aryan purity as preserved in the beautiful English women he chose to paint would import to his own work some of the quality of great Greek art. English womanly

4.4. Frederic Leighton, *Venus Disrobing*
Courtesy of Jeremey Mass & Co.

beauty conveys its pure Aryan superiority to the artist who depicts it, giving his paintings classical vitality.

The type of classical woman for which Leighton became known is languorous, and even when awake, she seems to be posing or pretending to be doing something rather than acting or moving. In many of his paintings, such as *Flaming June, The Garden of the Hesperides,* and *The Summer Moon,* the women sleep.[31] Leighton's sleeping women in transparent draperies portray unconscious female eroticism. The weight of their draperies slows them, inhibiting any vital movement. Because they are unconscious, they seem neither to will their sexual appeal to others nor to have any desire of their own. Leighton muffles the danger of an active, desiring woman by showing her asleep.

Not all Leighton's classical women are reassuring, modest, asleep, or dead. While their monumentality might suggest timeless racial superiority, associated with Aryanism, their massiveness can appear ominous, disturbing, and even grotesque. In *Psamanthe* (1880, figure 4.5), for example, the sea nymph's body fills the canvas. With her back to the viewer, her solid and generously filled frame dominates a sea which provides a calm backdrop for her stonelike figure. Psamanthe's imposing form seems like an immense Buddha brooding over the sea. The outlines of her body are still and broad, the water calm, the horizon untroubled; only the intricate lines of drapery folds indicate agitation, extending to the sea waves to surround the nymph so that her sealike draperies associate her with oceanic vastness. The other point of movement is the nymph's strongly coiling hair, placed as a focal point in the canvas. Wrapped and turned and as intricately painted as the draperies, the coil, with its dark center in a visually prominant place, set in contrast with the lighter sky, suggests the female sex while the nymph's stolid, massive back closes off from the viewer any sign of human expression.

While not a conventional emblem, Psamanthe's hair, like Browning's circles, functions as an emblematic object separable from the nymph's body. Emblem writers describe a process of "spiritualization" characteristic of emblems, leading the viewer from the eye of sense to the eye of understanding. By interpreting the coiled hair as emblematic, the viewer understands Psamanthe as a being whose sexual core is labyrinthine, a whorl with a dark, even frightening, center. Psamanthe does not sleep, but her back protects the viewer from her possibly more frightening other side.

4.5. Frederic Leighton, *Psamanthe*
Reproduced with the permission of the National Museums and Galleries on Merseyside.

Leighton combines the motif of the sleeping woman (this time she is apparently dead) with the rescue theme in *Hercules Wrestling with Death for the Body of Alcestis,* the painting Browning praised. A dark-skinned naked Hercules combats a troubling black Death at one end of the long canvas while at the center the white Alcestis, elaborately draped, stiffly reposes upon a bier. The struggle between the hero and death occurs on the same plane with the woman. The coloration is dramatically if conventionally symbolic. Although Leighton's painting is not a symbolist painting, he employed principles similar to those of the symbolists to convey emotions. The white draperies of Alcestis' body are scarcely lighter than her skin, while the shadowy figure of death, obscured by Hercules' naked body, casts his dark wing and draperies over the right side of the picture.[32] Leighton repeats the motif of Death's wing from this rescue painting in his two Andromeda paintings. In both paintings, the wings become emblematic objects associated with death. In the Andromeda and Perseus paintings they cover horrible acts.

The Return of Persephone (figure 4.6), a rescue painting exhibited the same year as *Perseus and Andromeda* (figure 4.7) shows Mercury leading Persephone up from the depths to her mother, Demeter, whose welcoming arms meet the upstretched arms of her daughter. The dramatic painting shows Demeter outlined by a radiant light from the earth she fecundates in celebration of her daughter's return. The picture portrays a return to the mother, an escape from the subterranean sexuality of Hades. The rescue story in *Alcestis* and *Persephone* differs from *Perseus and Andromeda.* In *Alcestis* the woman is someone's else's wife, with no suggestion of an erotic relationship between hero and victim. The myth of Demeter and Persephone recounts a return to an early nonerotic love. Perseus' rescue of Andromeda is prelude to marriage, and the nakedness of the woman, contrasts markedly to heavily draped women—Alcestis, Demeter, and Persephone—of Leighton's other rescue paintings.

Leighton's two Andromeda paintings reveal a complex personal tension, revealing a private imaginative life of a supremely public painter. Leighton's two Andromeda paintings deploy a heroic solar hero above the wings of a mythical beast, but under those wings the painter places another, frightening nether world. Emblematic objects in the two paintings reinforce the sexual

4.6. Frederic Leighton, *The Return of Persephone*
Courtesy of the Leeds City Art Galleries.

meaning of this dark world. Of Victorian dragons Leighton's is the most overpowering; his Andromeda's body twisted and distorted, extends the conventional view of Leighton's chaste classicism.[33] Leighton's Andromeda paintings are more Gothic than classical, despite their classical theme. The apparent glorious surface signifies a danger covered rather than a serene mindless genius. As it had for other Victorians, the Andromeda myth called forth in Leighton a conflict about sexuality that he dramatized in his disturbing representation of the chained woman assaulted by a fire-spitting beast.

In the earlier painting, "*Perseus and Andromeda,* the maiden and monster dominate the canvas, while "*Perseus on Pegasus Hastening to the rescue of Andromeda* (1895–96, figure 4.8) portrays the hero's preparation for rescue. The later painting places the figures in a static, almost paralyzed, composition, while suggesting the desperately active theme of its title. The round canvas of *The Garden of the Hesperides* (1892) also conveys an explicitly ominous serenity. The immense fat snake that coils around the tree, guarded by the resting maids, magnifies Medusa's curls in *Perseus Hastening to the Rescue.* Medusa's snaky curls also suggest the danger of Psamanthe's hair were it uncoiled.

Leighton places Perseus sitting upon Pegasus in the center of the round canvas, like a medallion. Pegasus rears slightly, his head back, his dark wings frozen, pausing in mid-flight. Perseus raises his arm behind his lowered neck in a gesture that seems as much compositional as thematic, his arm balancing the bent wings and raised legs of his flying steed. The hero may be reaching back for an arrow from the quiver, but he apparently has no bow, although in the earlier picture Perseus, in a similar pose from another perspective, has just shot the arrow that pierces the monster's back. He is possibly reaching back to adjust his cape, or he may be about to beat the horse. The ambiguity of the hero's gesture adds to the impression of stasis in the picture, of a pose being

4.7. Frederic Leighton, *Perseus and Andromeda*
Reproduced with the permission of the National Museums and Galleries on Merseywide.

struck rather than an action being taken. Perseus and the flying horse float in a realm of heroic gesture, an ideal and idealized champion.

Elements in the picture disrupt its balance. Medusa's head hangs free (Leighton may have seen the Italian fresco where her shrunken head hangs placidly, like a purse, from the hero's sword.) Her expression is horrified, her mouth frozen open in mid-scream, while

4.8. Frederic Leighton, *Perseus Hastening to the Rescue of Andromeda*
Reproduced with the permission of the Leicestershire County Council Museum and Art Gallery.

the snakes that are her hair fall beneath the horse's body in tensed positions that suggest they still live. Medusa's head hangs under the wings of Pegasus, who sprung from the blood spilled at her decapitation. Not holding on to the horse, Perseus rides bareback, twisting his body while his left hand gingerly grasps the Medusa's head by its snakes. His expression is intense, determined, almost demented. The coast of Rhodes shows in the background, while the looming rocks of the foreground suggest the Gorgon's transforming power.

Perseus and Andromeda is even more disturbing than *Perseus Hastening,* suggesting a brutal sexual fantasy. From a golden aura at the top of the painting Perseus riding Pegasus witnesses a dark scene below. Leaning forward as Pegasus rears back, he has just shot an arrow into an immense monster. The extreme contrast of coloration between the bright light of the Perseus figure in the upper portion of the canvas and the dark browns and blacks of the monster and the surrounding rocks suggest a color symbolism not apparent in the intense colors of *Perseus Hastening,* recalling the color symbolism of *Hercules Wrestling*. Bursting from the sun whose light surrounds him like a nimbus, Perseus is a celestial radiance. As in the solar mythology of the linguist Max Müller, who also promulgated a creed of Aryanism,[34] Leighton's sun-god represents his version of Greece: "the sudden upleaping of a living source . . . scattering abroad the light." The rescuer is portrayed as a higher being who sends his arrow into the depths of a chasm.

Perseus, triumphantly heroic, associated with the sun, good, and beauty, is remote from the grotesque scene beneath him. Although sun-lit, the colors in Perseus' part of the canvas do not compete with the intense rust of Andromeda's hair and the flames issuing from the monster's mouth. The sky is a pale blue, while Perseus appears passionless, drained of color. He is almost bodiless, refined into the distant spiritual deity whose rays touch the earth, conveying life. Unlike other Victorian representations, the hero does not descend from his celestial realm for direct contact with either beast or maiden. Man and woman are drastically separated in the picture. Perseus will feel no spray of the sea or dragon blood. There is no intimacy in Leighton's rescue, as there is in Rossetti's or Burne-Jones'. An utterly impersonal rescuer, Perseus sends a missile to slay the beast.

Leighton is the only Victorian who imagines the dragon slaying by means of bow and arrow. Perseus has already shot one seemingly ineffectual arrow which protrudes between the dragon's two mammoth wings. With its back pricked by the arrow, the dragon twists his neck to glower upward at the source of irritation and interruption. Connecting the lower part of the painting to the upper, the arrow, as a conventional sign of love, reinforces the symbolic meaning of the scene in the chasm. Perseus shoots Cupid's arrow which, detached from its ordinary context in a chubby naked boy's little bow, supplements the erotic interpretation of the grisly scene below. In the same way as Psamanthe's coiled hair suggests the symbolism of a shell, the arrow functions as an emblematic object, like Browning's skull.

Andromeda and the monster occupy the dramatic center of the picture. The maiden's cruelly twisted body stands cowering in a space that cannot contain her upright form. Rather than a classical pose characteristic of most Victorian representations of the maiden, Leighton crushes Andromeda by means of a niche created by rock and monster, violently contorting her body from the waist up. The niche does not enhance or frame Andromeda's beauty, as in Poynter's *Andromeda,* but assaults her. Her head twists back and sideways, utterly covered and shadowed by the beast, whose wing also covers her. The rest of her body, the utterly naked upper half, is grotesquely tortured. The lines of her shoulder, neck, and head echo the curve of the monster's neck and head. Her cascading red hair falls to the right, balancing the monster's wavy tail on the left. The monster's wings echo diabolically Pegasus' celestial wings.

Symbolically in the monster's shadow, Andromeda suffers under its emblematic infernal wing. In addition, the monster's horny legs straddle the twisted maiden. She has been partially incorporated by it. Torn from her upper body her draperies fall around her hips and are rendered with an attention to their graceful lines and creases, as in other of Leighton's classical paintings. The dramatic change between the halves of the figure symbolically splits the woman—in painting style and in color. Rather than convey classical control, the brightly lit draperies, out of the shadow of the monster, reproduce both the creased monster legs enveloping her and the rocks surrounding them.

The Ormonds describe the relationship between the figures in *Perseus and Andromeda* as "uneasy" and as not so successful as the later painting of Perseus, Medusa, and Pegasus, but it is precisely the unease which is the emotion conveyed.[35] Leighton brilliantly portrays one Victorian attitude about the bestial incivility of the sexual act. Irrational emotions disturb the classical pleasure of aesthetic control. The dragon enters Leighton's classical world with its beautiful Aryan ideal, separates man from woman, and tortures the woman, wresting her from classical drapery. Associated with heroism, Perseus cannot enter the depths to rescue her. He sends an emblematic arrow of Eros which, like Eden's apple, signifies the encounter of maiden and monster, an encounter of pain and domination rather than of pleasure and the serene joy that Leighton claimed was Greece's legacy.

Leighton places Andromeda's rock within a passageway that surrounds her with high craggy cliffs. In the background and through the legs of the monster, one catches a view of the open sea. The landscape in *Perseus and Andromeda* was painted in Ireland on the Donegal coastline, which Leighton described as "Dantesque in its grim blackness."[36] The name of the Irish place, "Malin Head," appropriately suggests the malign nature of what is happening in the painting and also "maidenhead."[37] The rocky canyon into which Leighton places Andromeda creates a polarity between the celestial sun where Perseus dominates his mythologically winged charger and the diabolic winged dragon who dominates the writhing woman. Andromeda struggles amidst a landscape which Leighton associates with Dante's morally lost realm. She is chained to a rock inside that realm, while Perseus remains on high, safe in his paradise.

Leighton's painting combines a cosmological, a moral, and a sexual mapping. Richard and Leonée Ormond notice sexual symbolism, but seem reticent to do more than suggest its possible meaning: "The monster . . . is truly a nightmarish creation. The way in which his huge scaly body rests almost on top of Andromeda, the black shape of its nearest wing forming a canopy, has almost obscene connotations."[38] In a later essay they avoid specificity by observing "something of the ancient sexual symbolism of the legend is evident here."[39] Whatever the ancient sexual symbolism may be, it does not inhere in the myth but is constructed by the Victorian painter. Leighton's sexual symbolism is not ancient in the sense of antique; it is primal. His return to this Greek myth uncovers a monstrous and violent sexual fantasy.

Although other Victorians, such as the Aesthetics, interpreted the myth as a sexual fantasy, they included elements of sanctity, intimacy, and possible pleasure along with their fears, curiosity, and possible inadequacy. Burne-Jones, for example, presents an intimate battle, and Poynter, in a lost painting, depicts an enormous winged creature, against which Perseus' sword seems puny as it pokes into the monster's mammoth open mouth.[40] But in both those paintings the hero bodily confronts the enemy. Leighton avoids an invidious comparison of hero to his enormous monster by the vast space between them.

Although the monster dwarfs Andromeda, he does not diminish the prominence of her body. Whereas the monster's horny skin blends with a similar texture in the rocks, Andromeda's luminous flesh foregrounds her twisted body and what is happening to it. Perseus' arrow shooting into the top of the monster's body suggests the obscene activity that is happening beneath it. Like Aesthetic representations, where the dragon becomes both male and female, Leighton's monster embodies male and female in the sexual act. The act being performed encompasses various kinds of fantasies, all of monstrous domination—eating, voiding, torture. The obscenity of the imagining suggests why Leighton portrayed his hero floating coldly aloof in the cool sky.

Highlighting the maiden and the obscenity of the monster's straddling position is a gap through which the distant sea glimmers, placid and remote. Along with the rocky promontory in the extreme foreground of the painting, that gap gives the painting a perspective into a mysterious event in a strangely enclosed world. Leighton had noted the effect of such a perspective: "Strange delightfulness of a far distant view seen thro' an arch or opening—particularly if this view be vague—the fascination of the *beyond.*"[41] Leighton's note suggests the pleasure of a forbidden looking, a spying into what cannot be known. The arch in *Perseus and Andromeda,* because of what creates it and what it encloses, is no ordinary opening. The distant view is delightful and vague while the grotesque happening in the uncomfortably close foreground, in the grim space that the gap outlines, suggests the frightening specifics of the concrete view.

In Leighton's painting the shapes in the landscape function as emblematic images, detachable symbolic objects that reinforce the painting's sexual meaning. The phallic-shaped promontory on which Andromeda and the monster stand projects into a canal-shaped inlet. Along with the arrow and the niche, emblems of man and woman respectively, the promontory pushing into the inlet, like Rossetti's stem forcing its way into the monster, signifies the forced encounter of woman and beast. These emblems, out of scale, perhaps magnifications and projections onto inanimate nature, provide an interpretative gloss on the picture, analogous to the glossing text of conventional emblems.

Taken together, the elements in Leighton's picture convey bestial sexuality. The monster squats over the twisted woman, the rough rock penetrating into the dark watery passage. The crazed monster with its gleaming red eye ravages the maiden in a symbolic representation of a fantasy of sexual activity that is violent, hideous, and frightening, combining scatological and scoptophilic elements. Neither languid nor aesthetic, the painting does not soothe with a drowsy aura as does the Hesperides painting, for example, where Leighton incorporates the potential danger of the huge snake into decorative rhythms. *Perseus and Andromeda* could not be described by Christopher Wood as "chaste, aesthetic, decorative, and evocative,"[42] as he characterizes Leighton's classical work, although the painting contains many motifs of Leighton's other more serene classical paintings. The disquiet of the picture suggests that Leighton, like the other Victorians who represented the myth, discerned a sexual conflict in the story that he expressed in the discontinuities between the classical and grotesque style of the maiden's body.

Leighton's private correspondence only gives hints about Leighton's representation of repulsive sexuality. Although the painter's letters to his "dearest Mammy" frequently express a vague notion that he might marry, he eventually explained to her that "I have never seen a girl to whom I felt the least desire to be married for life."[43] Writing as an artist, Leighton locates the desire to marry in his visual sense, but at the same time his words distance and aestheticize desire. In another letter, however, again to his mother, he associates marriage with his birthday: "Many thanks, dearest Mammy, for your kind wishes and congratulations on that melancholy occasion, my birthday—it is a day I always hate—fancy my being *thirty*!!!"[44] Leighton associates his birthday with becoming older, an unaesthetic process, but he also connects his birthday with marriage. Like Etty, Leighton vows not to marry, but he gives his mother theoretical reasons, as he associates his own birthday with marriage:

> About marrying, dear Mamma, you must not forget it takes two to play at that game. I would not insult a girl I did not love by asking her to tie her existence to mine, and I have not yet found one that I felt the slightest wish to marry: it is no doubt ludicrous to place this ideal so high, but it is not my fault—theoretically I should like to be married very well.[45]

Marriage is a tie, a bondage for life. "Theoretically" Leighton is interested, but the fleshly actuality has never slightly tempted him.

The painting's horror at a violent sexuality that is being imaged in the confrontation of monster and maiden perhaps illuminates the painter's objections to any actual prospect of marriage. Distancing himself from sexuality, generation, birthdays, the purest of his Aryan classicism avoids the confrontation he depicts in *Perseus and Andromeda*. The rescue scene of *The Return of Persephone* shows the maiden being returned to her mother from a subterranean, supernatural sexuality that began with abduction and rape. The rocks out of which Persephone emerges resemble the dark malign landscape in which Andromeda is trapped. To return to an earlier time for Leighton suggests as it does for Pater a return to themes of generation and birth. Leighton's public self kept aloof from those imaginings; his involvement with his favorite model, Dorothy Dean, although disruptive to her life, apparently did not involve the physical confrontation that he painted her as suffering in *Perseus and Andromeda*.

Disraeli (like Leighton, an elevated Peer of Victoria's realm) wickedly portrays Leighton in *Lothair* as Gaston Phoebus, "the most successful, not to say the most eminent, painter of the age."[46] Phoebus, an Appollonian type, propounds an Aryan theory which is completely self-referential in the narcissistic sense of advertizing its proponent.[47] "I have a conviction that among the great races the old creeds will come back," said Mr. Phoebus, "and it will be acknowledged that true religion is the worship of the beautiful."[48] Everything Phoebus does is aesthetic, performed in the radiant knowledge that he is one of the beautiful: "He had a belief, not without foundation, that everything was done better under his roof than under that of any other person."[49] He owns an island devoted to the re-creation of his aesthetic creed where everything is Aryan.

Like Leighton's own self-aware *Self-Portrait* of a rare beauty in which the copy of the Elgin marble behind him echoes the flesh tones of his own face, Phoebus thinks everything refers to his wonderful self. If Leighton indeed imagined sexuality as he presented it in painting the Andromeda myth, the emphasis upon the public life at the expense of the private one has a certain poignancy. His tiny private spaces in Leighton House contrast dramatically with the elaborate reception rooms which held wonderful concerts and public gatherings. In the light of Leighton's *Perseus and Andromeda,* James' portrayal of an artist without a private life suggests a fastidious aestheticism. The other side of his public persona, which Browning could identify with his own reluctance to reveal any intimate details of his private life, exposes a private grim fantasy. His painting of Andromeda's torment, with its avoidance of intimacy and the horrors it portrays—the twisted naked woman, the draperies surrounding her from the waist down, the Malin head rocks towering above her, the beast assimilating her, the hero avoiding the entire scene—affords an instance of Leighton depicting sexual conflict. The Victorian Andromeda myth provides the age with a code for expressing discomfort about gender and sexuality. Presenting his *Perseus and Andromeda* as an emblematic revelation, as did Robert Browning, Frederic, Baron Leighton of Stretton, the age's radiant icon of official art, gives the myth one of its most powerful and sinister interpretations.

EPILOGUE

The Gender Economy

ICTORIAN INTERPRETERS of the Perseus and Andromeda myth played the plot's happy balance of conventional gender polarities against more varied but more controversial gender definitions. The age could adore the ideal rescuer and his destined mate yet on some level suspect its own worship of them. Beneath the armor of Perseus' courage lay evidence of his vulnerability, while Andromeda's exemplary pliability might also indicate intractable mystery, a refusal to be known, or a fierce independence outside any male-ordained gender system. The Victorians discussed in previous chapters employed interpretative methods that explored the problematics rather than the fixities of their apparently rigid gender economy, although choosing to interpret this particular myth by means of a particular hermeneutic method set limits on the degree to which they could challenge that economy.

John Ruskin's belief in the myth exemplifies its interpretative possibilities for the age. Perhaps the associative tendency that became a sign of increasing madness also freed him from choosing one interpretative method over another. Toward the end of his life the most figural interpreter of his time embraced many contradictory meanings of the myth while holding fast to an ideal story by which to measure its manifestations. His brilliant polyvocal mind thus illustrates the multiple, even contradictory, interpretative possibilities of the Perseus and Andromeda myth when assimilated into the legend of St. George. The most piercing reader of historical periods by means of its figurations used the image of St. George as a test of a period's morality.[1] Ruskin's finely calibrated sensorium registered representation against changing social realities. Thus, Ruskin's words of the 1870s and '80s fittingly conclude my survey of the various ways in which the Victorian Andromeda myth becomes a cipher for expressing various tensions and inconsistencies of the Victorian gender system.

Ruskin presented a critique of a contemporary representation of St. George which he contrasts to the Saint's truest story, heard by the knights of the middle ages: "They [Richard Coeur-de-Lion and Edward III] must have heard some other story;—not, perhaps, one written down, nor needing to be written. A remembered story,—yet, probably, a little truer than the written one; and a little older."[2] This finest St. George legend, beyond written language, fueled his imagination. In postulating this ur-legend, Ruskin comes close to recognizing that all the interpreters of the Andromeda myth create a personal story, never before depicted in quite that way, from their own needs.

On the basis of his fantasy of the best medieval tale, Ruskin built a social dream. To combat the evils resulting from the vast societal changes of his times, he conceived of a rescue myth on an epic scale. Britannia herself was endangered by the evils of industrialized materialism, and Ruskin, with his Saint George's Guild and his fortune, set out to liberate her. Believing in St. George concretely, Ruskin quixotically attempted to transform the saint's miracle into life. He imagined that St. George's example could lead the way to combating those specific ills of his present time. Like Kingsley, he believed that St. George could be resurrected in the hearts of Victorians. The dragon's foul breath polluted the green and pleasant land, and so Ruskin called for a crusade, enlisting Companions as loyal followers of the Master, a "Son of St. George," as he perhaps unconsciously described himself, "a man desirous of setting the world to rights, if it might be, but not knowing the way of it."[3]

In spite of the Guild's failure, Ruskin remained in thrall to the myth, depending upon his vision of it to support both sides of his conflict between humanistic and religious interpretation. His thoughts increasingly returned to the Perseus/St. George myth as a vision of inspiration and as a way of assuring himself that all dragons could be vanquished. The duality of the hero—both Greek humanist and Christian martyr—highlighted and seemed to resolve the conflict between unconversion and reconversion.[4] When the researches of an Oxford student, James Reddie Anderson, revealed to him the connection between the Christian St. George and the antique Perseus, where the classical and Christian worlds meet, his faith in the myth's timeless truth momentarily arrested the fragmenting pull between Christian eschatology and humanistic utopianism:

> when I first read the legend of St. George . . . my eyes grew wet with tears of true delight; first, in the knowledge of so many beautiful things, at once given to me; and then in the surety of the wide good that the work thus begun would spring up into, in ways before wholly unconceived by me. (26 January 1878)[5]

Ruskin edited and published Anderson's essay which connects Perseus/Andromeda to St. George/Princess ("It does not merely resemble,—it *is* that story")[6] and interprets a Carpaccio *Saint George* in St. George's Chapel in St. Mark's according to the myth's revealed truth. The importance of Anderson's interpretation lies in its deployment of an eclectic blend of interpretations, separately discussed in previous chapters. Like Leighton, he finds that Perseus and St. George are associated with the sun. Like Hopkins, he gives the dragon an allegorical interpretation, associating it with

Spenser's monster and "the lust of the flesh."[7] He interprets the myth allegorically, typologically, and emblematically.

Anderson uses classical and Christian dimensions of the myth, considering Andromeda/Sabra an essential component of the St. George legend, as did his mentor. She is essential because her plight encourages the hero's valor and also because "her gratitude to this captain of the army of salvation and to the captain's Captain"[8] confirms the importance of the womanly role of abiding in faith, without running away or expressing terror, in a patient wait for salvation. Like Andromeda, the Princess is offered as a sacrifice for her people, but unlike the pagan princess, the Christian one required only faith: "If not willing, she was at least submissive; not for herself did she dream of flight. No chains in the rock were required for the Christian Andromeda."[9] Unlike pagan Andromeda, the Christian's chains are her duty, and she embraces her fate as a bride her groom.

Anderson turns the maiden into an allegorical figure, representing the "soul of man":

> This maiden, then, is an incarnation of spiritual life, mystically crowned with all the virtues. But their diviner meaning is yet unrevealed, and following the one legible command, she goes down to such a death for her people vainly. Only by help of the hero who slays monstrous births of nature . . . may she enter into that liberty with which Christ makes His people free.[10]

Although the maiden personifies man's higher element, she cannot perform rescue. Anderson seems partly aware that his exegesis was leading him to allow woman too powerful a role, a fulfillment of her name. In the gender and hermeneutic economy, Andromeda must remain a passive figure. She cannot be a ruler of men. By almost giving her great power, Ruskin's pupil seems close to acknowledging that the revival of this myth, particularly in a Christian context, represses a fantasy of great female power. His interpretation illustrates that the gender politics of interpretation—even with the combined hermeneutic power of various methods—can only toy with the possibility of a different power configuration for man and woman.

Ruskin's student verges on giving the Princess more power than her rescuer, while Ruskin's discussion of a representation of St. George indicates that the Victorian hero's power may be theatrical posing. As Ruskin's moral aesthetic exposed the debased representations of Bond Street Andromedas, so his moral economics revealed a weakened St. George in the marketplace of male exchange. Ruskin shows that Andromeda's chains, limiting woman to her assigned helplessness, also bind man to ineffectual heroic postures.

By examining a St. George on English coinage, Ruskin delineates the hero's helplessness. The design, by Benedetto Pistrucci, first appeared on an 1820 crown piece and later, fittingly, on a Jubilee sovereign, with Victoria on the other side (figure E.1). In the late 1870s the design seemed flawed, open to skeptical interpretation. Although Ruskin's critique of the artist's rendition was intended as a symbol of the inadequacy of current economic theory and its devastating effects, his subtext casts aspersions on the hero's manliness. The problem in the representation was neither aesthetic nor technical but conceptual:

> As a piece of mere die-cutting, that St. George is one of the best bits of work we have on our money. But as a design,—how brightly comic it is! The horse looks abstractly into the air, instead of where precisely it *would* have looked, at the beast between its legs: St. George, with nothing but his helmet on (being the last piece of armour he is likely to want), putting his naked feet, at least his feet showing their toes through the buskins, well forward, that the dragon may with the greatest convenience get a bite at them; and about to deliver a mortal blow at him with a sword which cannot reach him by a couple of yards.[11]

Except for flowing cape, helmet, and buskins, St. George is naked. Ruskin's reading of the St. George seen by more Victorians than any other undermines the heroic gestures of the rescue fantasy. Ruskin believed that the Princess was a proper part of the story, but here she has disappeared from consideration.[12] Eliminating the vulnerable woman from the myth reveals the precar-

E.1. Benedetto Pistrucci, "St. George" on English coinage. Queen Victoria on gold sovereign.
Courtesy of the Numismatic Collection, Yale University.

iousness of masculine heroism, a reminder of the possibility of female power. Ruskin pointed out that the hero's chivalric accutrements cannot possibly vanquish the monster. St. George's sword is too short to perform its heroic task, while his inadequate gear exposes his toes to the dragon's terrible teeth. Even his horse, as a component of the hero's power, is unaware of "the beast between his legs."[12] Ruskin's English George is not merely effeminate. Naked like Andromeda and vainly costumed in a useless cape, he is emasculated.

OVID FIGURES Andromeda first as an artifact to her rescuer's eyes. Perseus tells the liberated maiden that he mistook her for part of the rock to which she was chained. But, as I have argued, Ovid's Perseus was correct in his original apprehension. The maiden, celebrated by Roman and Victorian alike, is a cultural construct. Ovid's allusion to the created apparition, looming on the face of a rock, the quintessential sculptor's material, marks her true origins in the male artist's imagination; she is a paradigmatic aesthetic sign of the male culture's creation of woman.[13]

The Victorian myth portrays the helplessness of women and their need for protection in the face of increasingly strong opposing stories and growing evidence to the contrary. It presents the helpless maiden as a permanent truth against a changing and evolving reality. By counseling men against rape and women against ambition, it promises an eternity as a heavenly constellation.

For all of its appeal and its loving reiteration, however, the Victorian myth of Perseus and Andromeda cannot be thought of as resolving gender difficulties and the consequent social upheavals. Yet in its nondiscursive, nonrational presentation, the myth does have some effect. It defines the bounds of transgression, repressing the fear of unchained women by its appeal to a different order in which marriage effectively controls the ruler of men. Its Victorian reiterations indicate that it polices a boundary of social behavior, but its very repetitions indicate that the boundary has not been safely secured. Victoria herself was not exempt from the myth's terms; she acted them out, and when her Prince was no longer alive to contain her passionate will to rule, her extravagant mourning effectively removed her from the public sphere.

Pater's meditation on the meaning of Victorian classical revival with which I began this inquiry affirms that repression is necessary for any revival. Although the myth was a charm, its repetitions offering protection against unheroic knowledge, Victorian interpretation frequently brought that repressed fear to the surface. Throughout the age, the Andromeda myth's value in promising that the sexes were two distinct kinds kept its stock secure. By Victoria's first Jubilee in 1887 the naked hero waving an inadequate weapon could remind consumers of the symbol of female potency on the other side of the coin. In that age of democratic materialism, the myth's contradictory value passed from pocket to pocketbook as a coin of the realm.

Notes

Introduction: Interpretation and Gender

1. I present my argument for feminist interpretation of male literary works in "Notorious Signs, Feminist Criticism and Literary Tradition," *Making a Difference,* pp. 239–59.

2. Research into myth was a controversial Victorian field in which mythographers proposed theories based not only on mythographic tradition but also on the developing social sciences of anthropology, archaeology, psychology, and sociology. A full bibliography of Victorian mythographers would be too extensive, but see Feldman and Richardson, *The Rise of Modern Mythology.* For an overview of methods and definitions in myth research, see Doty, *Mythography.*

3. Sayce, *The Principles of Comparative Philology* (London 1874), p. 320n, quoted in Kissane, p. 13.

4. Pater, "Poems by William Morris," *The Westminster Review,* rpt. Sambrook, ed., *Pre-Raphaelitism,* p. 105.

5. *Ibid.*, p. 111.

6. Kestner, *Mythology and Misogyny,* argues that Victorian classical paintings reveal widespread misogynistic and gynophobic attitudes. He claims that this art emphasized female passivity and heroic male self-assertion. Kestner's book supports my conclusions, but unfortunately was not published until my own study had been completed.

7. As discussed by psychoanalytically oriented critics, this primary desire is always ambivalent, a mixture of attraction and repulsion. Theories of the effects of this primal mother central to the work of Dorothy Dinnerstein, Nancy Chodorow, Melanie Klein and the object relations school, Jacques Lacan, and Julia Kristeva have influenced my thinking about Pater's analysis of the significance of the classical revival.

1. *The Poetics of Rescue, the Politics of Bondage*

1. See Curran, "The Political Prometheus," *Studies in Romanticism,* and for Percy Shelley's transformations of Aeschylus, see Curran, *Shelley's Annus Mirabilis.*

2. Byron, "Prometheus," p. 31.

3. Shelley, Preface to *Prometheus Unbound,* p. 121.

4. Falk, "Elizabeth Barrett Browning and Her Prometheuses," discusses the progress and ultimate rejection of Elizabeth Barrett Browning's fascination with the Prometheus myth, suggesting that the woman poet could not adequately identify herself with the hero and still find a voice for herself.

5. Keats, "If by dull rhymes," p. 278.

6. Farmer, *The Dictionary of Oxford Saints,* p. 166, reports on the bridal dress; Delaney, *Dictionary of Saints,* attributes the marriage to a later accretion.

7. MacKinnon, "Toward Feminist Jurisprudence," p. 635. In the first part of MacKinnon's exploration of feminist inquiry, "Feminism, Marxism, Method, and the State: An Agenda for Theory," she states: "Ultimately, the feminist approach turns social inquiry into political hermeneutics . . . A feminist political hermeneutics would be a theory of the answer to the question, What does it mean? that would comprehend that the first question to address is, To whom? within a context that comprehends gender as a social division of power" (p. 24). For "social inquiry," I would substitute "cultural inquiry" to indicate the focus of my examination of the Victorian's Perseus and Andromeda myth. My inquiry seeks to make readable the power of traditional hermeneutic methods.

8. Bettleheim, *The Uses of Enchantment,* p. 111.

9. "Picture to yourself, my dear F," Dickens wrote to John Forster in 1849 from Rockingham Castle, "a large old castle, approached by an ancient Keep, portcullis &c, &c, filled with company waited on by six-and-twenty sevants; the slops (and wine glasses) continually being emptied; & my clothes (with myself in them) always being carried off to all sorts of places & you will have a faint idea of the mansion in which I am at present staying." *The Letters of Charles Dickens,* 5:661.

10. Huntington MS. 12/7/57, quoted in Johnson, *Charles Dickens,* 2:911.

11. Kaplan, "Bleak Houses: Charles Dickens at Home," p. 16; Edgar Johnson, "Breaking Point," 2:904–10.

12. Freud describes a misremembered scene from Alphonse Daudet's *Le Nabab* in which a poor bookkeeper rescues a great personage from a runaway horse and carriage, finding that the fantasy expressed his own need to be rescued: "I frequently walked about the streets, lonely and full of longings, greatly in need of a helper and protector." *Psychopathology of Everyday Life* (1901), 6:149.

13. Rape and rescue are not mutually exclusive, as shown in Ariosto's *Orlando Furioso,* where Ruggiero prepares to ravish Angelica, whom he has just rescued, when an exigency of the plot prevents him.

14. For a list of similar rescue paintings, see Casteras, *The Substance and the Shadow,* p. 71.

15. John Guille Millais, *The Life and Letters of Sir John Everett Millais,* 2:24. Millais points out that *The Knight Errant* is the only nude painting his father ever exhibited, a fact that supports a sexual interpretation. The woman's averted gaze turns into erotic desire when the mouth is painted slightly opened, and this suggestion of desire is augmented in Millais' painting by the suggestion of rape. Her desires have been loosened by her sexual experience, a fantasy that is expressed in some of the reviews which praise the knight and suggest that the woman may tempt him. See Nead, "Representation, Sexuality, and the Female Nude," pp. 234–36.

16. Freud, "A Special type of Choice of Object Made by Men," 9:173.

17. Ovid, Book IV, *Metamorphoses,* pp. 112–13.

18. The interpretation of passive women as expressing a passive element of the male psyche is found in Jungian psychology and in critics influenced by his formulations. See, for example, Stevenson, "The 'High-Born Maiden' Symbol in Tennyson"; Joseph, "Tennyson's Three Women." From a social perspective, Vicinus, in her introduction to *The Widening Sphere,* attributes idealization of female passivity to some males'

ambivalence about predominating definitions of masculinity (xviii). In the same collection Christ, in "Victorian Masculinity and the Angel in the House," argues that the ambivalence toward male aggression shown by Coventry Patmore and Alfred Lord Tennyson accounts for their idealization of female passivity.

19. Eliot, *Daniel Deronda,* Book 1, ch. 1. References will be given by book and chapter number in parentheses in the text.

20. Wolff, "George Eliot, Other-wise Marian Evans," pp. 36–38.

21. Benjamin, "The Bonds of Love," explores the dynamic of bondage, considered as love, as a basis for gender arrangements and as also manifested in pornography.

22. Ruskin, *Fors Clavigera,* 26:488–89.

23. A feminist perspective on respectable art, such as that undertaken by Gubar, "Representing Pornography," argues that we cannot isolate aesthetic from pornographic experiences and Caws, "Ladies Shot and Painted," considers the perverse image in later depictions of women who are fragmented and rearranged. Griffin, *Pornography and Silence* argues that the pornographic mind dominates our culture" (pp. 2–3).

24. See Ortner, "Is Female to Male as Nature Is to Culture?," for an anthropological perspective on the identification of woman with nature.

25. Auerbach, *Woman and the Demon,* describes the power of the woman in paintings and literature as a repressed energy that surfaces by representing them as outcasts. Andromeda's chains are a different sign of controlling woman's energy, threat, and danger.

26. Girard, "Shakespeare's Theory of Mythology," p. 109.

27. In speculating on how gender becomes constructed, Cucchiari, "The Origins of Gender Hierarchy," has influenced my thinking about multiple gendered possibilities in the Andromeda myth.

28. For an extended analysis of Medusa and Perseus, see Tyrrell, *Amazons,* p. 109.

29. Slater, *The Glory of Hera,* points out that the snake is predominately a female symbol: "The snake appears far more often in mythology as a devouring than as a penetrating being, and when dragons appear in pairs, the female is almost always the more formidable of the two . . . The 'danger' arises, because the serpent, whether viewed as a genital or not, is orally defined, and the fear which it evokes is of being absorbed by the mother," p. 87. Slater's study has been useful to my own thinking about the relationship between family dynamics and symbolic process.

30. Malinowski, in "Myth in Primitive Psychology," explains this kind of resolution as a primary function of myth. For primitive peoples

myth "expresses, enhances, and codifies belief; it safeguards and enforces morality . . ." Myth, he finds, justifies inequalities, attaching itself to forms of social power or social claims. Even considering the added complexity of a myth revival and the complicated Western history behind it, Malinowski's insight is relevant to the social context of Victorian representation, which uses the Andromeda myth to justify inequalities by naturalizing the social fact of masculine dominance. See also Dumezil, *The Destiny of a Warrior:* "The function of that particular class of legend known as myth is to express dramatically the ideology under which a society lives," p. 3.

31. Tyrrell, *Amazons,* describes the Greek polarization of genders in his discussion of the myth of the Amazons. Divided into positive and negative elements, woman's (positive) fertility is controlled by marriage and her (negative) capacity to act on her own is contained by patriarchal marriage: "Marriage is a fundamental structure of male order," p. xix. Tyrrell's method of addressing the construction of the Amazon myth in a cultural context has informed my own thinking. Particularly suggestive is his discussion of myth as a symbolic representation of cultural conflict, his discussion of marriage, and his analysis of Perseus as a myth about the son's conflicts.

32. *Queen Victoria in Her Letters and Journals,* Hibburt, ed., p. 152.

33. Girouard, *The Return to Camelot,* documents the dangers inherent in the chivalric ideal. Dijkstra's survey of European *fin de siècle* representations of women demonstrates how the "medusan" woman and man's fear of her dominates later mythologies.

34. Gilbert and Gubar, *The Madwoman in the Attic.*

2. *Manly Allegories*

1. *Charles Kingsley: His Letters and Memories of his Life,* p. 82. Fanny Kingsley heavily edited the memoir which is nonetheless invaluable. Subsequent references to it appear as *LM* in parentheses in the text. With the exception of his lectures and reviews, references to other Kingsley works are taken from the 19 volume edition of the collected works and are indicated by volume number in parentheses in the text.

2. I do not mean that allegorical representations are only rational. Hinks' distinctions in *Myth and Allegory* defines the rational process necessary to allegory. Applied to the analytical process of interpretation, allegory meant the technique of extracting the metaphysical notions in a complex of imagery (pp. 2–3). Hinks also distinguishes between mythical and allegorical thinking. In allegory as opposed to myth: "Conscious reflexion,

not intuition alone, is responsible for the choice of the symbol and its precise metaphorical significance" p. 13.

3. Kingsley, "Sacred and Legendary Art," p. 222.

4. Fowler, *Kinds of Literature,* p. 192.

5. The defeat of Benjamin Haydon over the decoration of the Houses of Parliament signaled the demise of history painting's empire. For a brief review of the controversy, see Bell, *Victorian Artists,* pp. 18–20, an account biased against Etty and Frost. Treble, "The Palace of Westminster Decorations," pp. 92–93, offers a bibliography and summary of the controversy about genres.

6. Opie, Lecture 1, *Lectures on Painting,* pp. 7–8.

7. See Berger, *Ways of Seeing,* on the sexual appeal of the allegorical painting to the spectator/owner, particularly pp. 54–57.

8. Curtius, in *European Literature and the Latin Middle Ages,* addresses changes in style, the use of the *topos,* and the merging of the classical and Christian canon; Seznec, in *The Survival of the Pagan Gods,* categorizes the ways legends were justified to accord with Christian doctrine. Fowler, in *Kinds of Literature,* links this process to what he calls "allegorical modulation" p. 192.

9. Although allegory arises at the same time in literary and iconographic criticism, there has been a tendency to privilege verbal over visual allegory. See Hinks, p. 12. G. E. Lessing's *Laocoön* (1766) describes the making of personifications into allegorical figures by means of attributes. These attributes are not needed by the poet, he says, because the poet can simply name the personification. Lessing is part of that romantic denigration of allegory examined by de Man in "Rhetoric of Temporality," which does not address visual allegory. Northrup Frye, *Anatomy of Criticism,* p. 90, calls personification "naive allegory," which he defines as "the translation of ideas into images." Quilligan, in *The Language of Allegory,* writes about literary narratives.

10. Gaunt and Roe, *Etty and the Nude,* p. 17.

11. Gilchrist, *The Life of William Etty,* p. 36.

12. *Ibid.,* p. 235.

13. From the 1843 notebook, quoted in Bailey, *William Etty's Nudes,* p. 25.

14. *Ibid.,* pp. 65–66.

15. *Ibid.,* p. 36.

16. Farr, *William Etty,* quotes a review from *The Times* of January 1822: "Naked figures, when painted with the purity of Raphael, may be endured: but nakedness without purity is offensive and indecent, and in Mr. Etty's canvases is mere dirty flesh" (p. 31).

17. Gilchrist, *The Life of William Etty,* p. 318.

18. Farr, *William Etty,* pp. 88–89.

19. Ripa, *Baroque and Rococo Pictorial Imagery,* no. 58.

20. Marcus, *The Other Victorians,* p. 274.

21. Stoller, *Perversion.*

22. Sandby, *History of the Royal Academy,* p. 221.

23. For a brief review of Frost's illustrations of Milton see Treble, *Great Victorian Pictures,* p. 38.

24. DeLaura in "Hopkins and Carlyle," points out doctrinal differences between Hopkins and the muscular Christians, calling Kingsley "hysterical" in comparison to Hopkins' " 'ecstasy' of love," p. 75.

25. October 12, 1881, *The Correspondence,* p. 74.

26. Cucchiari in "Origins of Gender Hierarchy," points out that an institution does not only reflect a cultural construct but it also reproduces it. Marriage is both an expression and a defense of the gender hierarchy. "The symbolic expression of male dominance [marriage] does not merely reflect the gender hierarchy, however; it also causes and actively maintains that hierarchy," p. 62.

27. *The Poems of Gerard Manley Hopkins,* 71, "Harry Ploughman." Henceforth references will be cited by poem number and title in parentheses in the text.

28. White, "Harry Ploughman's Muscles," p. 31.

29. April 27, 1881, *Letters to Robert Bridges,* p. 127–28.

30. *Stonyhurst Magazine,* Nov. 1888, p. 236; qtd. in Roberts, "The Countryman as Hero," p. 80.

31. *Further Letters,* p. 386.

32. *Spiritual Exercises of St. Ignatius,* p. 1.

33. Chitty, *A Life of Charles Kingsley,* Letter #53, 1843, p. 59. Hereafter referred to as Chitty in parentheses in the text.

34. Benjamin, in "The Bonds of Love," argues that the fantasy of erotic domination permeates sexual imagery in our culture. Gender is created by the male splitting off his emotional life, overvaluing rationality and by the female accepting subordination, overvaluing submission. The outlines of master-slave fantasies are drawn. The Andromeda myth fills in the outline more benevolently, for the monsters bear some of the sadomasochistic elements. Nonetheless, Kingsley's idea of taming the maiden by using her sexual desire compares to the portrayal of O from *The Story of O* as being initiated sexually into bondage, discussed by Benjamin.

35. October 15, 1866, *Further Letters,* p. 31.

36. Democratically opening the aristocratic code of chivalry to com-

mon men, Kingsley shifts emphasis from military and social status to conduct. His revision of chivalric activity combined with social conscience forms the basis of manly Christianity. See Vance, "Varieties of Manliness," pp. 8–28, and Girouard, "Muscular Chivalry," pp. 132–44.

37. For reproductions of some drawings, see Chitty.

38. ". . . that longing to get rid of walls and roofs and all the chrysalis case of humanity is the earnest of a higher, richer state of existence. That instinct which the very child has to get rid of clothes, and cuddle to flesh—what is it but the longing for fuller union with those it loves?" (*LM,* 2:201).

39. DeBeauvoir, *The Second Sex,* pp. 144–45.

40. Ortner, "Is Female to Male as Nature Is to Culture?," pp. 67–88, discusses woman's place in the gender hierarchy which Kingsley's drawing illustrates.

41. Dinnerstein, "The Dirty Goddess," pp. 124–56, discusses consequences to culture of representing woman as carnal scapegoat-idol, and connects this ancient practice to cultural violence, a pattern discernible in Kingsley's placement of Woman.

42. For a description of the split subject in Kristeva's analysis, see Roudiez's "Introduction" to *Desire in Language,* p. 6.

43. Prestige structures (social honor or value) depend upon symbolic associations that rationalize ordering of human relations. Ortner and Whitehead, "Accounting for Sexual Meanings," p. 14.

44. Auerbach, *Woman and the Demon,* discusses the unconscious empowerment granted women by allowing them to dominate the picture plane. Not only does Kingsley give to Woman and Andromeda this dominance, but he acknowledges it. Although one frequently discovers, as here, that the man seems to cede dominance to the woman while actually keeping control, it is also true that on another level, the male sees himself as less powerful in regard to Woman. It is this conflict and the violence of its terms that partly constitutes Kingsley's love of active manliness and his delight in depicting women's martyrdom.

45. See Dinnerstein, "Mama and the Mad Megamachine," pp. 207–26; Chodorow, "Mothering, Masculinity, and Captalism," pp. 180–90; Rich, "Mother and Son, Woman and Man," pp. 186–217.

46. Fletcher goes even further: "I would maintain that ritualized rhythm is enough by itself to render exposition symbolic." *Allegory,* p. 169.

47. Rubin, "The Traffic in Women," pp. 157–210.

48. For a psychological interpretation of *The Water Babies* in terms of

Kingsley's concern with bathing, see Carpenter, "Parson Lot takes a cold bath," pp. 23–43.

49. Kingsley, *Literary and General Lectures and Essays,* pp. 187–228.

50. *Ibid.,* p. 203.

51. *Ibid.*

52. *Ibid.,* p. 259.

53. Kingsley, "The Poetry of Sacred and Legendary Art," p. 225, but see also, "The Water Supply of London," pp. 199–236.

54. Kingsley compares the polishing of his verse with keeping his clothes clean: "There is no more reason in not polishing, than there is for walking about with a hole or a spot on your trousers, a thing which drives me mad. If I have a spot on my clothes, I am conscious of nothing else the whole day long" (*LM,* 1:84).

55. Kingsley, *Miscellanies,* 2:317.

56. Douglas warns against psychoanalytic interpretations which do not consider the social need to maintain the culture. Rituals of cleanliness and pollution, for example, may have a private (neurotic) meaning, but the rituals of purification also serve a public purpose. Douglas cautions, "The rituals enact the form of social relations and in giving these relations visible expression they enable people to know their own society. The rituals work upon the body politic through the symbolic medium of the physical body," *Purity and Danger,* p. 124. For Kingsley, marriage is a purification ritual, congruent with the social relations the Andromeda myth represents.

57. Following the standard four-fold way of medieval reading, Boccaccio allowed that Perseus slaying the Medusa could be interpreted literally, morally, or allegorically. The allegorical interpretation most relevant to Hopkins is that Perseus is a symbol of Christ. See Seznec, p. 223.

58. Ross, *Mystagogus Poeticus,* p. 360.

59. Milward, *A Commentary on the Sonnets,* cites "piece" as Shakespearean, and also attributes to the word a sexual meaning: "At stake is her flower of maidenhood," p. 73.

60. Harris, *Inspirations Unbidden,* cites the cannibalism of the imagery in "Carrion Comfort" as a perversion of communion, p. 124.

61. See *Further Letters,* p. 18.

62. Houghton, *Victorian Frame of Mind,* pp. 99–106, extends authoritarian attitudes beyond religious matters.

63. Pater, *Greek Studies,* p. 2.

64. Pater, "Demeter and Persephone," *Greek Studies,* p. 96.

65. *Ibid.*, pp. 98–99.

66. *Ibid.*, p. 151.

67. Turner, *The Greek Heritage,* places Pater's theory in context, pp. 77–134.

68. August 14, 1879, *Letters to Bridges,* p. 87.

69. Hughes, ed. *Paradise Lost* p. 250 n., quotes St. James (i,15) "When lust hath conceived, it bringeth forth sin: and sin, when it is finished, bringeth forth death" as the text allegorized by Athena's birth. Athena is Perseus' protector; such interweaving of myth and interpretations over the centuries gives Hopkins' poem its resonances.

70. According to Sulloway, *Hopkins,* Hopkins considered Spenser's Saint George the ideal type of gentleman, p. 124.

71. Hopkins did not always imagine the dragon as female. A meditation on dragons written during Long Retreat on November 8, 1881, shows that he identified the dragon of Revelation as male: "The snake or serpent is symbol of the Devil. So also the Dragon. A dragon is or is taken to be a reptile. And first a dragon is a serpent. . . . So that if the Devil is symbolised as a snake he must be an archsnake and a dragon . . . And therefore I suppose the dragon as a type of the Devil to express the universality of his powers, both the gifts he has by nature and the attributes and sway he grasps, and the horror which the whole inspires." *Sermons and Devotional Writings,* p. 199.

72. Quilligan, *Milton's Spenser,* traces and interprets the traditions from which this allegorizing comes and points to Spenser's depiction of the cannibalistic progeny who, in the allegorical interpretation, feed upon their mother: sin feeds upon itself: "Spenser invests the scene with a cannibalistic progeny so self-destructively greedy as to pose no threat to the hero" (p. 82).

73. *Ibid.*, p. 88.

74. *Ibid.*, p. 81.

75. Harrison, *The Dark Angel,* p. 73.

76. November 19, 1879, *Further Letters,* p. 243.

77. January 19, 1879, *Letters to Bridges,* p. 61.

78. Patmore, Canto XII, *Husband and Wife,* I. "The Married Lover," p. 146.

79. September 24, 1883, *Further Letters,* p. 310.

80. *Ibid.*

81. Patmore, "The Weaker Vessel," p. 6.

82. *Ibid.*

83. Kitchen, *Gerard Manley Hopkins,* suggests that Hopkins "no doubt became conscious that he did not live up to the Victorian ideal" (p. 35)

of manliness. His worship of manliness becomes a poignant vision of the Christ as chevalier, giving the worshipper an impossible goal for a middle name.

3. Typologies of Defloration

1. *Letters of Dante Gabriel Rossetti,* 1:109.

2. Of the many studies of the uses of Victorian typology, the ones most relevant to these particular figures are Landow, *Victorian Types;* Sussman, *Fact Into Figure;* Stein, *The Ritual of Interpretation.* The study of typology I have found most useful is Charity, *Events and Their Afterlife.*

3. Hunt, *The Pre-Raphaelite Imagination,* compares the Pre-Raphaelites to Symbolists: "This translation of idea into plastic fact is an exact and thoughtful art; it was often beyond the Pre-Raphaelite imagination. For despite Rossetti's insistence on poetry's fundamental brainwork, the Pre-Raphaelites tend to respond intuitively and emotionally to the resources and depths of human experience which their symbolism chooses to celebrate" p. 29.

4. Kristeva, "Stabat Mater," pp. 99–118, discusses the consecrated representation of woman, describing how man's identity as flesh is only made human through the maternal. Her discussion clarifies the importance to Dante Gabriel Rossetti of the typological connection between the Virgin and Andromeda to confirm his male identity.

5. Buchanan, *The Contemporary Review,* p. 343.

6. *Ibid.*

7. Busst, "The Androgyne," argues that any meaning of the androgynous image is dependent upon the historical context: "We must . . . come to the conclusion that both exterior and interior sources of the image of the androgyne play little part in determining its meaning or value in any particular work: these depend uniquely on the preoccupations and convictions, ideals and aspirations of the individual artist or author which, if not always those of his whole generation and civilization, are at least largely conditioned by his upbringing and environment," p. 10.

8. Landow, in *Victorian Types,* discusses how Rossetti secularizes typology, using it to give coherence to his own life, p. 179.

9. Culler, "Studies in Rossetti's Reading."

10. Heywoode, *Gynaikion,* p. 267.

11. Rossetti, *Poetical Works,* p. 89. Further references to this edition will be cited by page number in parentheses in the text.

12. Vasari's biography of Raphael portrayes the painter as amorous:

"Raphael kept up his secret love affairs and pursued his pleasures with no sense of moderation," p. 320.

13. Panofsky defines pseudomorphosis as being more than reinterpretation: "While classical images were thus deliberately reinterpreted, there are many other cases in which the revived classical traditions merged quite naturally, or even automatically, with surviving medieval traditions. When a classical character had emerged from the Middle Ages in utterly nonclassical disguise . . . and had been restored to its original appearance by the Renaissance, the final result often showed traces of this process. Some of the medieval garments or attributes would cling to the remodelled form, and thereby carry over a medieval element into the content of the new image.

"This resulted in what I would like to call a 'pseudomorphosis'; certain Renaissance figures became invested with a meaning which for all their classicizing appearance, had not been present in their classical prototypes, though it had been foreshadowed in classical literature" (pp. 70–71).

14. Pater, "Poems by William Morris," p. 112.

15. *Ibid.*

16. *Ibid.*

17. "Dante Gabriel Rossetti," p. 218. I use early unrevised versions of Pater's essays, particularly when he excised relevant passages in later editions.

18. *Ibid.*, p. 218.

19. Using psychoanalytic theory, Carroll, *The Cult of the Virgin Mary,* argues that male interest in the Virgin denotes a "strong but strongly repressed desire for the mother" in a social class with ineffectual fathers. Moers, *Literary Women,* p. 105, aruges that there was sibling erotic nursery play in the Rossetti family. Moers' insight is corroborated by a hint of their father (who, like the men in Carroll's study, failed to earn a living) in a begging letter: "my family has got to such a stage that it is necessary at all costs to separate the boys from the girls" (December 1835). Waller, *The Rossetti Family,* p. 125.

20. Quoted from Grieve, *The Art of Dante Gabriel Rossetti,* p. 8.

21. Pater, "Dante Gabriel Rossetti," p. 220.

22. Grieve, *The Pre-Raphaelites,* p. 73.

23. Grieve uses this term which I have not encountered anywhere else, but I adopt it as being descriptive of the verbal equation between the flower and defloration.

24. W. M. Rossetti, *Family Letters,* 1; 160.

25. I have been unable to discover why Rossetti chose June in this

poem, whereas *Ecce Ancilla Domini* bears the date "March 1850" to accord with the official date of the Annunciation.

26. Nochlin, "Lost and Found," discusses Angelica as a prisoner of sex and reads the tenor of every metaphor as sexual.

27. The *OED* defines "teraphim" as both singular and plural of Hebrew origin, referring to idols or images, or an idol or image (2:3263). Milton uses it unfavorably in the plural and Donne uses it as a singular noun referring to a false god.

28. Ariosto, Canto X, xcvi, 2; 161.

29. Sedgwick, *Between Men,* offers yet another perspective on the complex gendered actions that occur at the moment of slaying. According to Sedgwick's model, the female would be the ostensible reason for the rescue, but the object of desire, that which draws the male, is the (male) monster. The violent passionate action which then occurs is between the monster and the hero.

30. Freud, "The Taboo of Virginity" (1917), 11:193–208.

31. Pater, "Poems by William Morris," p. 106.

32. Morris, *The Collected Works,* 1:1–2.

33. *Ibid.,* 3:169. Page numbers to this volume appear in parentheses in the text.

34. See Praz, "The Beauty of the Medusa," pp. 25–50, for the blending of beauty and sadness.

35. Gitter, "Victorian writers were fascinated not only by the problem of 'reading' women's hair—interpreting its meaning and exploring its symbolic value—but also by the hair itself," p. 941.

36. McGann, "The Beauty of the Medusa," p. 20.

37. Slater, *The Glory of Hera,* discusses the threat of the Medusa as the power of the mother: "The Perseus myth . . . reflects a social system in which the father is peripheral in the home, and in which emotional power is seen as residing in the mother. It is she who must be confronted, and when Perseus wishes to vanquish his enemies the only way he can think to do it is by exposing them to the same maternal bogie which so terrifies him" (p. 31).

Slater identifies this maternal bogie as the Medusa's head, representation of the mother's genitals. Slater, however, emphasizes the mother's desire whereas I am placing more emphasis on the son's desire. His description of a peripheral father accords with Carroll's description of the family dynamics which give rise to the cult of the Virgin Mary.

38. Gitter, "Women's Hair," pp. 941–42.

39. Kestner, "Edward Burne-Jones," pp. 95–122.

40. Harrison and Waters, *Burne-Jones,* p. 31.

4. *Celestial Emblems*

41. Photographic Collection, Warburg Institute, University of London.

42. For a discussion of the typological system which includes classical myth as well as the Old Testament, see Seznec, *The Survival of the Pagan Gods.*

43. See Harrison and Waters, *Burne-Jones,* plate 29, p. 25, for a sketch of Burne-Jones and Morris at work in their Red Lion studio, with the brass rubbing tacked to the wall.

44. The calm of Burne-Jones' picture contrasts sharply with Caravaggio's painting of the Medusa on a shield-shaped round canvas. Caravaggio expresses the horror and violence of Perseus' decapitation of her. The Gorgon shrieks, while the blood pours from her severed neck, in contrast to the paralysis in Burne-Jones' picture.

45. For a discussion of snake-like monsters as women, see Adelman and for representations of women, snakes, and multiple possibilities of signification, see Dijkstra, pp. 305–13.

46. Pater, "Wincklemann," *The Renaissance,* p. 213.

47. Swinburne, "The Poems of Dante Gabriel Rossetti," 15:3.

48. Wilde, "The Artist as Critic," p. 391. One finds sameness in difference, Wilde paradoxically asserts. But the difference becomes sameness, resulting in androgyny in sex and in translation in language, both experiments in Otherness.

4. *Celestial Emblems*

1. Browning, *Balaustion's Adventure,* Kenyon, ed., vol. 7, 2673–75.

2. James, p. 191.

3. La Sizeranne, *La Peinture,* p. 133 (my translation).

4. Browning, John Pettigrew, ed., p. 347. Unless otherwise specified subsequent line numbers of Browning poems in the text will be from this edition.

5. Loy Martin's inquiry into the production of Browning's monologues influences my description of modern subjectivity.

6. James, pp. 196–97.

7. Kristeva, in "The Bounded Text," *Desire in Language,* describes how the semiotic sign is "dualist, hierarchical, and hierarchizing." Signs become "reified universals, . . . objects in the strongest sense of the word" (p. 40).

8. DeVane, "The Virgin and the Dragon," pp. 33–46.

9. Browning, *Cornhill,* 1902, p. 152, letter to Katharine Bronson, quoted in *Learned Lady,* p. 25.

10. Barrett Browning, "Two Autobiographical Essays," p. 123.

11. Creston, *Andromeda in Wimpole Street.*

12. Barrett Browning, *Poems,* p. 354.

13. No. 9, February 26, 1845,, *Letters of Robert Browning and Elizabeth Barrett Barrett,* p. 27.

14. Segal, "Envy," *Introduction to the Work of Melanie Klein,* p. 41.

15. The witch curling around the god is another of Browning's enclosures, described by Eleanor Cook, *Browning's Lyrics,* pp. 109–11.

16. See p. 1024 notes to Pettigrew/Collins edition for the identification "radiant form" with a Shelleyan locution. See also Harold Bloom on the relationship between Shelley and Browning. I find particularly useful Bloom's discussion of daemonization and negation of the precursor from the *The Anxiety of Influence,* pp. 100–3, although Bloom's own repression of female influence in general leaves out that crucial aspect of Browning's poetic identity.

17. In "Troops of Shadows," I argue that the title *Pauline* refers to Browning's replacing Shelley by means of Pauline typology. The pun on Percy exemplifies a similar transformation and replacement occurring in the poem. In his overdetermined use of the Andromeda myth, Browning also replaces the male Shelley with the female Andromeda/Elizabeth, a figure he can both reject and appropriate.

18. Cook, p. 109, connects the chains in this passage to Browning's imagery of enclosure, thus giving imagistic support to the connection of the witch curled around the god and Andromeda's chains.

19. DeVane, *Browning's Parleyings,* p. 167.

20. Dieckman, *Hieroglyphics,* p. 68.

21. Roppen, *Evolution and Poetic Belief,* questions Browning's claims to be sympathetic with evolution and finds them in the Platonic tradition, pp. 171 ff.

22. Beer, *Darwin's Plots,* pp. 24–26.

23. For a discussion of the ouroboros as a female sign, see Dijkstra, *Idols of Perversity,* pp. 128–29, and *passim.* Dijkstra emphasizes the decadent uses of the symbol as "the circle of chaos with a woman's body" (p. 129) and the womanly desire to "physical self-reproduction." Browning uses the symbol as a transcendent healing one to stave off the masculine danger of the serpent. Although the ouroboros does not terrify Browning, it is a female sign, and one could not consider his resolution any less ambiguous or subtle than "resolutions" in his earlier poems. Claiming a female symbol for his own can never be an utter triumph.

24. In addition to Kristeva, see Cixous, "The Laugh of the Medusa," p. 247, and Duras, "From an Interview," p. 174.

25. Leighton, *Addresses Delivered to the Students of the Royal Academy,* p. 85.

26. Letter to Emilia Frances Pattison, Aug. 9, 1879, BM Add. MS. 43907, ff. 134–36, quoted in Ormond, *Lord Leighton,* p. 85.

27. See Landow, "Victorianized Romans," for a discussion of a similar domestication of Latin themes. George Hersey, "Aryanism in Victorian England," makes a similar point about Leighton's paintings and also noticed the deliberate conflation of Victorian and Greek maidens, attributing it to Leighton's eclectic style and to his Aryanism.

28. Harrison, *The Dark Angel,* asserts that the woman covering herself "convey[s] a sense of shame calculated to soothe male fears and gratify the masculine thirst for superiority" (p. 82) and mocks the sense of discomfort this picture shows. The self-consciousness of Venus conveys the self-consciousness of her creator.

29. Leighton, pp. 86–87.

30. *Ibid.,* p. 89.

31. Wood, *Olympian Dreamers,* p. 64. Wood does not find anything disturbing the surface brilliance of Leighton's classical paintings.

32. Wood, p. 33, describes the symbolist elements of *Hercules* as a precursor to some of his later pictures in regard to their mood of restlessness and tension.

33. Dijkstra, in *Idols of Perversity,* catalogues the *fin de siècle* contortions of female bodies and attributes those representations to fear of women. He mentions Leighton's sleeping figures as exhausted, "collapsing woman" (pp. 72–73); Leighton anticipates in other ways the violent depictions of tortured and torturous women that Dijkstra attributes to a later age.

34. Müller, *Chips from a German Workshop,* vol. 2, *Essays on Mythology, Traditions, and Customs.* Turner, "Max Müller—Myth as the Disease of Language," pp. 104–115, discusses Max Müller's solar mythology in relation to his Aryanism and his linguistic theory: "The sun had been the central object of interest to the ancestors of the Aryans . . . the words originally simply descriptive of the sun eventually came to have narrative stories associated with them. . . . Although Müller considered his theory applicable to all Aryan myths, he drew most, though not all, of his examples from the Greek myths (p. 107).

35. Ormond, "Victorian Painting and Classical Myth," p. 38.

36. Ormond, *Lord Leighton,* p. 120.

37. See Ormond (1975) Catalogue, p. 476. *Rocks: Malin Head, Donegal* and 477. *Malin Head, Donegal,* p. 176. The authors identify the lost

sketch (476) as a "study for the background of *Perseus and Andromeda,* which the plate of 477 would seem to verify.

38. Ormond, *Leighton,* p. 127.

39. Ormond, "Classical Myth," p. 38.

40. Photograph from the *Art Journal* reproduced in Wood, *Olympian Dreamers,* pp. 140–41.

41. Ormond, *Leighton,* p. 130.

42. Wood, *Olympian Dreamers,* p. 70.

43. Barrington, *Frederic Leighton,* 2:56.

44. *Ibid.*

45. *Ibid.*

46. Disraeli, *Lothair,* p. 131.

47. Hersey interprets Leighton's aesthetic theory as ultimately narcissistic. The artist, he claims, recommends all art as a metaphor for the self. Although Hersey exaggerates Leighton's emphasis upon self-portraiture in all art: "When one does not see one's self, in short, one sees nothing" (p. 109), he usefully indicates the quality in all of Leighton's painting that makes it seem narrow, almost self-referential.

48. *Lothair,* p. 373.

49. *Ibid.,* p. 176.

Epilogue: The Gender Economy

1. Helsinger, *Ruskin and the Art of the Beholder,* discusses Ruskin's theory of art as language.

2. Ruskin, Letter 26 (February 1873), *Fors Clavigera, Works,* 27:478.

3. Ruskin, "The Sword of St. George," *Fors Clavigera, Works,* 27:290.

4. For the connections between the Guild and Ruskin's madness, see Rosenberg, *The Darkening Glass,* pp. 196 ff.

5. Ruskin, *St. Mark's Rest,* XI. "The Place of Dragons," *Works,* 24:371.

6. *Ibid.*

7. *Ibid.,* p. 386.

8. *Ibid.,* p. 396.

9. *Ibid.,* p. 396.

10. *Ibid.,* p. 398.

11. *Fors Clavigera,* 27:474–75.

12. Ruskin's source for this belief was *The Famous Historie of the Seaven Champions of Christendome, Saint George of England, etc.,* by Richard Johnson, first published in 1616. See *Works,* 24:246, n.1.

13. For a formulation of the construction of gender that considers the

complicity of women and the control of men in defining the system, see Flax, "Postmodernism and Gender Relations:" "gender relations are complex and unstable processes . . . constituted by and through interrelated parts. These parts are interdependent, that is, each part can have no meaning or existence without the others" (pp. 628–29).

Bibliography

Adelman, Janet. *The Common Liar: An Essay on Antony and Cleopatra.* New Haven: Yale University Press, 1973.

Ariosto, Lodovico. *The Orlando Furioso.* William Stewart Rose, trans. London: John Murray, 1824.

Auerbach, Nina. *Woman and the Demon: The Life of a Victorian Myth.* Cambridge: Harvard University Press, 1982.

Bailey, Brian J. *William Etty's Nudes.* Bedford: Inglenook Press, 1974.

Barrington, Mrs. Russell. *The Life, Letters, and Work of Frederic Leighton,* vol. 2. London: George Allen, Ruskin House, 1906.

Beauvoir, Simone de. *The Second Sex.* New York: Bantam, 1961; rpt. Knopf, 1952; rpt. Librairie Gallimard, 1949.

Beer, Gillian. *Darwin's Plots: Evolutionary Narrative in Darwin, George Eliot, and Nineteenth-Century Fiction.* London: Routlege & Kegan Paul, 1983.

Bell, Quentin. *Victorian Artists.* Cambridge: Harvard University Press, 1967.

Benjamin, Jessica. "The Bonds of Love: Rational Violence and Erotic Domination." In Hester Eisenstein and Alice Jardine, eds., *The Future of Difference,* pp. 41–70. New Brunswick: Rutgers University Press, 1985.

Berger, John. *Ways of Seeing.* Harmondsworth: Penguin, 1973.

Bettleheim, Bruno. *The Uses of Enchantment: The Meaning and Importance of Fairy Tales.* New York: Knopf, 1976.

Bloom, Harold. *The Anxiety of Influence.* New York: Oxford University Press, 1973.

Browning, Elizabeth Barrett. *Poems by Elizabeth Barrett Browning,* vol. 1. 3d ed. London: Chapman & Hall, 1853.

—— "Two Autobiographical Essays by Elizabeth Barrett." *Browning Institute Studies* (1974), 2:119–34.

Browning, Elizabeth Barrett and Robert Browning. *The Letters of Robert Browning and Elizabeth Barrett Barrett,* vol. 1. Elvan Kintner, ed. Cambridge: Harvard University Press, 1969.

Browning, Robert. *Learned Lady: Letters from Robert Browning to Mrs. Thomas FitzGerald, 1876–1889.* Edward C. McAleer, ed. Cambridge: Harvard University Press, 1966.

—— *Robert Browning: The Poems,* 2 vols. John Pettigrew, ed. New Haven: Yale University Press, 1981.

—— *The Works of Robert Browning,* vol. 7. (Centenary Edition) F. G. Kenyon, ed. London: 1912.

Byron, Lord. *The Complete Poetical Works,* vol. 4. Jerome J. McGann, ed. Oxford: Clarendon Press, 1980.

Buchanan, John. "The Fleshly School of Poetry: Mr. D. G. Rossetti. *The Contemporary Review* (1871), 18:334–50.

Busst, A. J. L. "The Androgyne." In Ian Fletcher, ed., *Romantic Mythologies,* pp. 1–95. London: Routledge & Kegan Paul, 1967.

Carpenter, Herbert. *Secret Gardens: The Golden Age of Children's Literature.* Boston: Houghton Mifflin, 1985.

Carroll, Michael P. *The Cult of the Virgin Mary: Psychological Origins.* Princeton: Princeton University Press, 1986.

Casteras, Susan. *The Substance and the Shadow: Images of Victorian Womanhood.* New Haven: Yale Center for British Art, 1982.

Caws, Mary Ann. "Ladies Shot and Painted: Female Embodiment in Surrealist Art." In Susan Rubin Suleiman, ed., *The Female Body in Western Culture,* pp. 262–87. Cambridge: Harvard University Press, 1986.

Charity, A. C. *Events and Their Afterlife: The Dialectics of Christian Ty-*

pology in the Bible and Dante. Cambridge: Cambridge University Press, 1966.

Chitty, Susan. *The Beast and the Monk: A Life of Charles Kingsley*. London: Hodder and Stoughton, 1974.

Chodorow, Nancy. *The Reproduction of Mothering: The Sociology of Gender*. Berkeley: University of California, 1977.

Christ, Carol. "Victorian Masculinity and the Angel in the House." In Martha Vicinus, ed., *The Widening Sphere: Changing Roles of Victorian Women,* pp. 146–62. Bloomington: Indiana University Press, 1977.

Cixous, Helen. "The Laugh of the Medusa." In Elaine Marks and Isabelle de Courtivron, eds., *New French Feminisms,* pp. 245–64. New York: Schocken Books, 1981.

Cook, Eleanor. *Browning's Lyrics: An Exploration*. Toronto: University of Toronto Press, 1974.

Creston, Dormer. *Andromeda in Wimpole Street*. New York: Dutton, 1930.

Cucchiari, Salvatore. "The Origins of Gender Hierarchy." In Sherry B. Ortner and Harriet Whitehead, eds., *Sexual Meanings: The Cultural Construction of Gender and Sexuality*. pp. 31–79. Cambridge: Cambridge University Press, 1981.

Culler, Helen Simpson. "Studies in Rossetti's Reading." Ph.D. dissertation, Yale University, 1943.

Curran, Stuart. "The Political Prometheus." *Studies in Romanticism* (1986), 25:429–55.

—— *Shelley's Annus Mirabilis*. San Marino, Huntington Library, 1976.

Curtius, Ernst Robert. *European Literature and the Latin Middle Ages*. New York: Bollingen 36, 1953.

de beauvoir, Simone. *The Second Sex*. New York: Bantam, 1961; rpt. Knopf, 1952; rpt. Librairie Gallimard, 1949.

Delaney, John J. *Dictionary of Saints*. London: Kaye & Ward, 1982.

DeLaura David. "Hopkins and Carlyle: "My Hero, My Chevalier." *The Hopkins Quarterly* (July 1975), 2:67–76.

de Man, Paul. "Rhetoric of Temporality." In Charles Singleton, ed., *Interpretation: Theory and Practice,* pp. 173–209. Baltimore: Johns Hopkins University Press, 1969.

DeVane, William C. *Browning's Parleyings*. New Haven: Yale University Press, 1927.

—— "The Virgin and the Dragon." *The Yale Review* (1947), 37:33–46.

Dickens, Charles. *The Letters of Charles Dickens,* vol. 5. Graham Storey and K. J. Fielding, eds. Oxford: Clarendon Press, 1981.

Dieckman, Lisolotte. *Hieroglyphics: The History of a Literary Symbol.* St. Louis: Washington University Press, 1970.

Dijkstra, Bram. *Idols of Perversity: Fantasies of Feminine Evil in Fin-de-Siècle Culture.* New York: Oxford University Press, 1986.

Dinnerstein, Dorothy. *The Mermaid and the Minotaur: Sexual Arrangements and Human Malaise.* New York: Harper, 1976.

Disraeli, Benjamin. *Lothair. The Bradenham Edition of the Novels and Tales of Benjamin Disraeli, 1st Earl of Beaconsfield,* vol. 11. New York: Knopf, n.d.

Doty, William G., *Mythography: The Study of Myths and Rituals.* University: Alabama University Press, 1986.

Douglas, Mary. *Purity and Danger: An Analysis of the Concepts of Pollution and Taboo.* London: Ark Paperbacks, 1984.

Dumezil, Georges. *The Destiny of a Warrior.* Chicago: University of Chicago Press, 1970.

Duras, Marguerite. "From an Interview." In Elaine Marks and Isabelle de Courtivron, eds., *New French Feminisms,* pp. 174–76. New York: Schocken Books, 1981.

Eliot, George. *Daniel Deronda.* Graham Handley, ed. Oxford: Clarendon Press, 1984.

Falk, Alice. "Elizabeth Barrett Browning and Her Prometheuses: Self-Will and a Woman Poet." *Tulsa Studies in Women's Literature* (1988), 7:69–85.

Farmer, David Hugh. *The Dictionary of Oxford Saints.* Oxford: Clarendon Press, 1978.

Farr, Dennis. *William Etty.* London: Routledge & Kegan Paul, 1958.

Feldman, Burton and Robert D. Richardson. *The Rise of Modern Mythology: 1680–1860.* Bloomington: Indiana University Press, 1972.

Flax, Jane. "Postmodernism and Gender Relations in Feminist Theory." *Signs* (1987), 12:621–43.

Fletcher, Angus. *Allegory: The Theory of a Symbolic Mode.* Ithaca: Cornell University Press, 1964.

Fowler, Alastair. *Kinds of Literature: An Introduction to the Theory of Genres and Modes.* Cambridge: Harvard University Press, 1982.

Freud, Sigmund. *The Standard Edition of the Complete Psychological Works.* 24 vols. James Strachey, trans. and ed. London: The Hogarth Press, 1953–74.

Frye, Northrop. *Anatomy of Criticism.* New York: Atheneum, 1968.

Gaunt, William and F. Gordon Roe. *Etty and the Nude.* Essex: F. Lewis, 1943.

Gilbert, Sandra and Susan Gubar. *The Madwoman in the Attic: The Woman*

Writer and the Nineteenth-Century Literary Imagination. New Haven: Yale University Press, 1979.
Gilchrist, Alexander. *The Life of William Etty, R.A.* 1855, rpt. EP Publishing, 1978.
Girard, René. "Shakespeare's Theory of Mythology." In *Classical Mythology in Twentieth-Century Thought and Literature,* Wendell M. Aycock and Theodore M. Klein, eds., pp. 107–24. Lubbock: Texas Tech Press, 1980.
Girouard, Mark. *The Return to Camelot: Chivalry and the English Gentleman.* New Haven: Yale University Press, 1981.
Gitter, Elisabeth G. "The Power of Women's Hair in the Victorian Imagination," *PMLA* (1984), 99:936–54.
Grieve, A. I. *The Art of Dante Gabriel Rossetti: The Pre-Raphaelite Period.* Norwich: Real World Publications, 1973.
—— *The Pre-Raphaelites.* London: Tate Gallery, Penguin Books, 1984.
Griffin, Susan. *Pornography and Silence.* New York: Harper Colophon, 1981.
Gubar, Susan. "Representing Pornography: Feminism, Criticism, and Depictions of Female Violation." *Critical Inquiry* (1987), 13:712–41.
Harris, Daniel A. *Inspirations Unbidden: The Terrible Sonnets of Gerard Manley Hopkins.* Berkeley: University of California Press, 1982.
Harrison, Fraser. *The Dark Angel: Aspects of Victorian Sexuality* London: Sheldon Press, 1977.
Harrison, Martin and Bill Waters, *Burne-Jones.* New York: Putnam, 1973.
Helsinger, Elizabeth. *Ruskin and the Art of the Beholder.* Cambridge: Harvard University Press, 1982.
Hersey, George L. "Aryanism in Victorian England." *The Yale Review* (1977), 66:104–13.
Heywoode, Thomas. *Gynaikion, or Nine Books of Various History Concerning Women.* London: Adam Islip, 1624.
Hinks, Roger. *Myth and Allegory in Ancient Art.* London: Warburg Institute, 1939.
Hopkins, Gerard Manley. *The Correspondence of Gerard Manley Hopkins and R. W. Dixon.* Claude Colleer Abbott, ed. London: Oxford University Press, 1955.
—— *Further Letters of Gerard Manley Hopkins.* Claude Colleer Abbott, ed. London: Oxford University Press, 1956.
—— *The Letters of Gerard Manley Hopkins to Robert Bridges.* Claude Colleer Abbott, ed. London: Oxford University Press 1955.
—— *The Poems of Gerard Manley Hopkins.* 4th ed. W. H. Gardner and N. H. MacKenzie, eds. London: Oxford University Press, 1967.

—— *The Sermons and Devotional Writings of Gerard Manley Hopkins.* Christopher Devlin, S.J., ed. London: Oxford University Press, 1950.

Houghton, Walter. *The Victorian Frame of Mind.* New Haven: Yale University Press, 1957.

Hunt, John Dixon. *The Pre-Raphaelite Imagination, 1848–1900.* Lincoln: University of Nebraska Press, 1968.

James, Henry. *The Complete Tales of Henry James,* vol. 8. Leon Edel, ed. Philadelphia: Lippincott, 1962.

Johnson, Edgar. *Charles Dickens: His Tragedy and Triumph.* New York: Simon and Schuster, 1952.

Joseph, Gerhard. "Tennyson's Three Women: The Thought Within the Image." *Victorian Poetry* (1981), 19:1–18.

Kaplan, Fred. "Bleak Houses: Charles Dickens at Home." *Thesis* (Fall 1986), 1:16–21.

Keats, John. *The Complete Poems of John Keats.* Jack Stillinger, ed. Cambridge: Harvard University Press, 1978.

Kestner, Joseph. *Mythology and Misogyny: The Social Discourse of Nineteenth-Century British Classical Painting.* Madison: University of Wisconsin Press, 1988.

—— "Edward Burne-Jones and Nineteenth-Century Fear of Women." *Biography* (1984), 7:95–122.

Kingsley, Charles. *The Life and Works of Charles Kingsley.* Fanny Kingsley, ed. 19 vols. London: Macmillan, 1901.

—— "On English Literature." In *Literary and General Lectures and Essays,* pp. 245–68. London: Macmillan, 1890.

—— "Sacred and Legendary Art." In *Literary and General Lectures and Essays,* pp. 187–228. London: Macmillan, 1890.

—— "Speech on Behalf of the Ladies Sanitary Association." In *Miscellanies,* 2:309–17. London: Parker, 1859.

—— "The Water Supply of London." In *Miscellanies,* 2:199–236. London: Parker, 1859.

Kissane, James. "Victorian Mythology." *Victorian Studies* (1962), 6:5–28.

Kitchen, Paddy. *Gerard Manley Hopkins.* New York: Atheneum, 1979.

Kristeva, Julia. "The Bounded Text." In *Desire in Language: A Semiotic Approach to Literature and Art.* Leon S. Roudiez, trans. New York: Columbia University Press, 1980.

—— "Stabat Mater," In Susan Rubin Suleiman, ed., *The Female Body in Western Culture,* pp. 99–118. Cambridge, Harvard University Press, 1986.

Landow, George P. *Victorian Types, Victorian Shadows.* Boston: Routledge and Kegan Paul, 1980.

—— "Victorianized Romans: Images of Rome in Victorian Painting." *Browning Institute Studies* (1984), 12:29–52.

La Sizeranne, Robert de. *La Peinture anglais contemporaine, 1844–1894.* Paris: Hachette, n.d.

Leighton, Lord Frederic. *Addresses Delivered to the Students of the Royal Academy.* Alexandra Orr, ed. London: Kegan Paul, Trench, Trubner, 1897.

Loyola, St. Ignatius. *The Spiritual Exercises of St. Ignatius.* Louis J. Puhl, S. J. trans. Westminster, Md.: Newman Press, 1959.

McGann, Jerome G. "The Beauty of the Medusa: A Study in Romantic Literary Iconology," *Studies in Romanticism* (1972), 11:3–25.

MacKinnon, Catherine A. "Feminism, Marxism, Method, and the State: An Agenda for Theory." In Nannerl O. Keohane, Michelle Z. Rosaldo, and Barbara C. Gelpi, eds., *Feminist Theory: A Critique of Ideology,* pp. 1–30. Chicago: University of Chicago Press, 1981–82.

—— "Feminism, Marxism, Method, and the State: Toward Feminism, Marxism, Method, and the State: Toward Feminist Jurisprudence." *Signs* (1983), 8:635–58.

Malinowski, Bronislaw. "Myth in Primitive Psychology." In *Magic, Science, and Religion and Other Essays.* Boston: Beacon, 1948.

Marcus, Steven. *The Other Victorians: A Study of Sexuality and Pornography in Mid-Nineteenth-Century England.* New York: Basic Books, 1964.

Martin, Loy. *Browning's Monologues and the Post-Romantic Subject.* Baltimore: Johns Hopkins University Press, 1985.

Millais, John Guille. *The Life and Letters of Sir John Everett Millais,* vol. 2. London: Methuen, 1899.

Milton, John. *Complete Poems and Major Prose.* Merritt Y. Hughes, ed. New York: Odyssey Press, 1957.

Milward, S. J., Peter. *A Commentary on the Sonnets of Gerard Manley Hopkins.* London: Hurst, 1970.

Moers, Ellen. *Literary Women: The Great Writers.* Garden City, N.Y.: Doubleday, 1976.

Morris, William. *The Collected Works of William Morris,* vols. 1 and 3. May Morris, ed. London: Longmans Green, 1910.

Müller, Max. *Chips from a German Workshop,* vol. 2. *Essays on Mythology, Traditions, and Customs,* 2d ed. London: Longmans, Green, 1868.

Munich, Adrienne. "Notorious Signs, Feminist Criticism and Literary Tradition." In Gayle Greene and Coppélia Kahn, eds., *Making a Difference: Feminist Literary Criticism,* pp. 239–59. London: Methuen, 1985.

—— "Troops of Shadows: Browning's Types." In Harold Bloom and

Adrienne Munich, eds., *Robert Browning: A Collection of Critical Essays,* pp. 167–87. Englewood Cliffs, N.J.: Prentice-Hall, 1979.

Nead, Linda. "Representation, Sexuality, and the Female Nude." *Art History* (1983), 6:234–36.

Nochlin, Linda. "Lost and Found: Once More the Fallen Woman." In Norma Broude and Mary D. Garrard, eds., *Feminism and Art History: Questioning the Litany,* pp. 221–70. New York: Harper and Row, 1982.

Opie, John. *Lectures on Painting.* London: Longmans, Hurst, Rees and Orme, 1809.

Ormond, Richard and Leonée Ormond. *Lord Leighton.* New Haven: Yale University Press, 1975.

—— "Victorian Painting and Classical Myth." *Victorian High Renaissance.* Minneapolis: Minneapolis Institute of Arts, 1978.

Ortner, Sherry B. "Is Female to Male as Nature Is to Culture?" In Michelle Zimbalist Rosaldo and Louise Lamphere, eds., *Woman, Culture, and Society,* pp. 67–87. Stanford: Stanford University Press, 1974.

Ortner, Sherry B. and Harriet Whitehead, "Accounting for Sexual Meanings." In Sherry B. Ortner and Harriet Whitehead, eds., *Sexual Meanings: The Cultural Construction of Gender and Sexuality,* pp. 1–28. Cambridge: Cambridge University Press, 1981.

Ovid. *Metamorphoses.* Mary M. Innes, trans. Harmondsworth: Penguin, 1955.

Panofsky, Erwin. *Studies in Iconology.* New York: Harper and Row, 1962.

Pater, Walter. "Dante Gabriel Rossetti." In *Appreciations, With an Essay on Style,* pp. 213–27. London: Macmillan, 1898.

—— *Greek Studies, The Works of Walter Pater,* vol. 7. London: Macmillan, 1901.

—— "Poems by William Morris," *The Westminster Review* (1868), rpt. in *Pre-Raphaelitism: A Collection of Critical Essays,* James Sambrook, ed., pp. 105–17. Chicago: University of Chicago Press, 1974.

—— *The Renaissance,* 2d ed. London: Macmillan, 1898.

Patmore, Coventry. "Why Women Are Dissatisfied." *St. James's Gazette* (1887), pp. 6–7.

—— "The Weaker Vessel." *St. James's Gazette* (1887), pp. 5–6.

—— *The Angel in the House. Poems,* vol. 1. London: George Bell, 1897.

Praz, Mario. *The Romantic Agony,* 1933, rpt. New York: Meridian Books, 1968.

Quilligan, Maureen. *The Language of Allegory: Defining the Genre.* Ithaca: Cornell University Press, 1979.

—— *Milton's Spenser: The Politics of Reading.* Ithaca: Cornell University Press, 1983.

Rich, Adrienne. *Of Woman Born: Motherhood as Experience and Institution*. New York: Norton, 1976.

Ripa, Cesare. *Baroque and Rococo Pictorial Imagery, the 1758–60 Hertel Edition of Ripa's Iconologia*. Edward A. Maser, ed. New York: Dover, 1971.

Roberts, Gerald. "The Countryman as Hero: A Note," *Hopkins Quarterly* (1982), 9:79–83.

Roppen, Georg. *Evolution and Poetic Belief: A Study in Some Victorian and Modern Writers*. Oslo: Oslo University Press, 1956.

Rosenberg, John D. *The Darkening Glass: A Portrait of Ruskin's Genius*. New York: Columbia University Press, 1961.

Ross, Alexander. *Mystagogus Poeticus, or The Muses Interpreter*. 1648 rpt. New York: Garland, 1976.

Rossetti, Dante Gabriel. *Letters of Dante Gabriel Rossetti,* 3 vols. Oswald Doughty and John Robert Wahl, eds. Oxford: Clarendon Press, 1965.

—— *The Poetical Works of Dante Gabriel Rossetti*. William Michael Rossetti, ed. London: Ellis and Elvey, 1903.

Rossetti, William Michael, ed. *Dante Gabriel Rossetti: His Family Letters, With a Memoir by William Michael Rossetti,* 3 vols. Boston: Roberts, 1895.

Rubin, Gayle. "The Traffic in Women: Notes on the 'Political Economy' of Sex." In Rayna R. Reiter, ed., *Toward an Anthropology of Women,* pp. 157–210. New York: Monthly Review Press, 1975.

Ruskin, John. *The Complete Works of John Ruskin*. 39 vols. E. T. Cook and Alexander Wedderburn, eds. London: George Allen, 1912.

Sandby, William. *History of the Royal Academy of Arts, From Its Foundation in 1768 to the Present Time*. London: Longman, Roberts, & Green, 1862.

Segal, Hannah. *Introduction to the Work of Melanie Klein*. New York: Basic Books, 1974.

Sedgwick, Eve Kosofsky. *Between Men: English Literature and Male Homosocial Desire*. New York: Columbia University Press, 1985.

Seznec, Jean. *The Survival of the Pagan Gods: The Mythological Tradition and Its Place in Renaissance Humanism and Art*. Princeton: Princeton University Press, Bollingen, 38, 1953.

Shelley, Percy Bysshe. *Prometheus Unbound,* A variorium edition. Lawrence John Zillman, ed. Seattle: University of Washington Press, 1959.

Slater, Philip E. *The Glory of Hera: Greek Mythology and the Greek Family*. Boston: Beacon, 1968.

Stein, Richard L. *The Ritual of Interpretation*. Cambridge: Harvard University Press, 1975.

Stevenson, Lionel. "The 'High-Born Maiden' Symbol in Tennyson." *PMLA* (1948) 63:234–43.

Stoller, Robert. *Perversion: The Erotic Form of Hatred*. New York: Random House, 1974.

Sulloway, Allison G. *Hopkins and the Victorian Temper*. London: Routledge and Kegan Paul, 1972.

Sussman, Herbert. *Fact Into Figure: Typology in Carlyle, Ruskin, and the Pre-Raphaelite Brotherhood*. Columbus: Ohio State University Press, 1979.

Swinburne, Charles Algernon. *Essays and Studies: The Complete Works of Algernon Charles Swinburne,* vol. 15. Sir Edmund Gosse and Thomas James Wise, eds. London: Heinemann, 1926.

Treble, Rosemary. "The Palace of Westminster Decorations." In *Great Victorian Pictures,* pp. 91–93. London: Arts Council of Great Britain, 1978.

Turner, Frank M. *The Greek Heritage in Victorian Britain*. New Haven: Yale University Press, 1981.

Tyrrell, William Blake. *Amazons: A Study in Athenian Mythmaking*. Baltimore: Johns Hopkins University Press, 1984.

Vance, Norman. *The Sinews of the Spirit: The Ideal of Christian Manliness in Victorian Literature and Religious Thought*. Cambridge: Cambridge University Press, 1985.

Vasari, Giorgio. *Lives of the Artists,* George Bull, trans. Harmonsworth: Penguin, 1965.

Vicinus, Martha. *The Widening Sphere: Changing Roles of Victorian Women*. Bloomington: Indiana University Press, 1977.

Victoria, Queen. *Queen Victoria in Her Letters and Journals,* Christopher Hibburt, ed. New York: Viking, 1985.

Waller, R. D. *The Rossetti Family, 1824–1854*. Manchester: Manchester University Press, 1932.

White, Norman. "Harry Ploughman's Muscles." *The Hopkins Quarterly* (1975), 2:29–31.

Wilde, Oscar. *Critical Writing of Oscar Wilde*. Richard Ellmann, ed. New York: Random House, 1968.

Wolff, Michael. "George Eliot, Other-wise Marian Evans." *Browning Institute Studies* (1986), 13:25–44.

Wood, Christopher. *Olympian Dreamers: Victorian Classical Painters: 1860–1914*. London: Constable, 1983.

Index

Page numbers in italics indicate art.